Shallow End

Ryan Gross

ISBN 978-1-970970-03-6

DEDICATION

For Doyle – I miss you

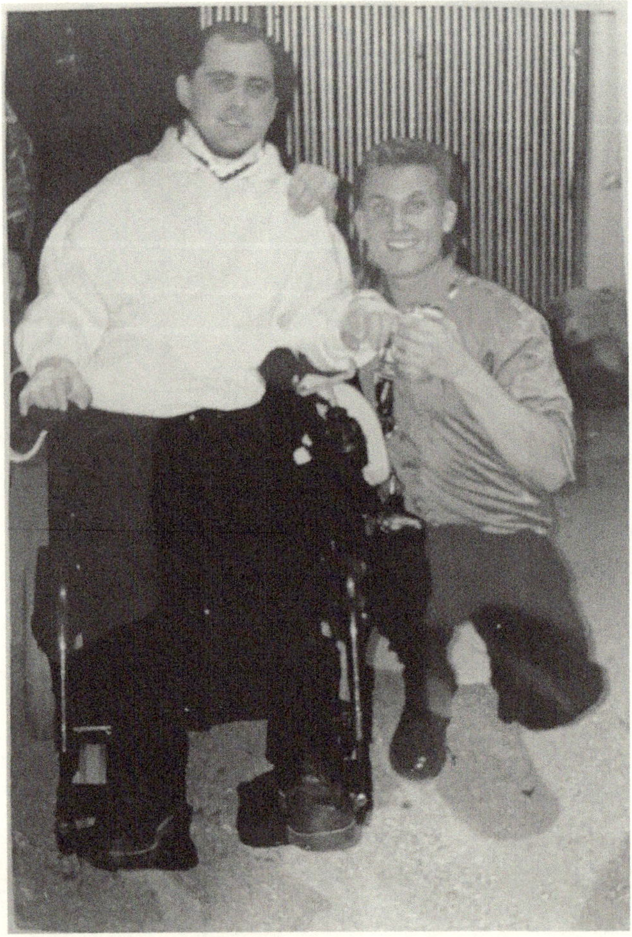

For the families... The ones who show up every day. Who learn to operate equipment they never wanted to understand. Who sleep in hospital chairs and fight with insurance companies while they advocate for their loved ones who no longer can. For those who change sheets and empty bags pretending not to notice the tears. Who carry the impossible weight and never complain because their loved one is carrying more. You are the unsung heroes of this story.

For healthcare providers... The nurses who remember names and preferences. The aides who work double shifts for wages that don't reflect their worth. The therapists who celebrate small victories and mourn the setbacks alongside their patients. The doctors who deliver devastating news and still find ways to offer hope. The caretakers who become family.

You chose to spend your lives easing the suffering of others. That choice matters more than you will ever know. For everyone who has ever fed someone who couldn't lift a fork. Bathed someone who couldn't reach the soap. Listened to someone who needed to rage against a body that betrayed them or held the hand of someone who couldn't hold back. This book is for you.

Your compassion does not go unseen.

Your sacrifice does not go unnoticed.

Your love does not go unfelt.

Author Note

This book is based on true events. Some names, identifying details, and locations have been changed to protect the privacy of individuals and their families. Certain conversations have been recreated from memory, and some events have been condensed or reordered for narrative clarity.

This is one man's recollection of another man's life and death. Memory is imperfect, shaped by grief, time, and the stories we tell ourselves to survive. I have done my best to honor the truth of what happened and, more importantly, the truth of who he was. This story contains depictions of catastrophic injury, chronic illness, and end-of-life decisions that some readers may find difficult.

This book of fiction is based on a true story.

To those living with spinal cord injuries and other catastrophic disabilities... I see you. I see the courage it takes to face each day when your body has become a prison. I see the exhaustion of depending on others for the most basic human dignities. I see the grief you carry for the person you were, for the future you lost and for the simple pleasures most people take for granted. A handshake. A hug. The ability to wipe your own tears.

Your pain is real. Your frustration is valid. Your anger is justified.

And if you've ever felt that the world would be better without you, or that ending your suffering is the only door left to open, please know this... I understand why you feel that way. I won't pretend to have easy answers or hollow reassurances. What I will say is that your life has meaning beyond what your body can do. You matter to people in ways you may never fully see.

To the families and loved ones... I see you too. I see the guilt that gnaws at you in quiet moments. The what-ifs that replay endlessly. The exhaustion of caregiving that no one talks about. The complicated grief of watching someone you love become different, in pain and slipping away while still breathing. You are not selfish for feeling overwhelmed. You are not weak for crying in the shower. You are not a bad person for sometimes wishing it would end, even as you hate yourself for the thought.

Loving someone through catastrophic disability is one of the hardest things a human being can do. It requires you to show up, day after day and to witness suffering you cannot fix. It asks you to be strong when you have nothing left. It demands that you hold space for someone else's despair while drowning in your own.

Some of you have lost someone. Maybe to the injury itself. Maybe to the slow erosion of hope or to a choice they made when the pain became too much to carry. If you're carrying that weight, please take care of yourself.

This book is not a manual for healing. It's not a guide to recovery or a roadmap through grief. It's simply a story about two friends, about what was lost, and about learning to carry the weight of that loss without letting it bury you. If you're struggling, please reach out. Talk to someone. You don't have to carry this by yourself.

Crisis Resources

988 Suicide & Crisis Lifeline: Call or text 988 (available 24/7)

Crisis Text Line: Text HOME to 741741

Veterans Crisis Line: Call 988, then press 1

International Association for Suicide Prevention:

https://www.iasp.info/resources/Crisis_Centres/

For Those Living with Spinal Cord Injuries:

Christopher & Dana Reeve Foundation: 1-800-539-7309 |

www.christopherreeve.org

United Spinal Association: 1-800-962-9629 | www.unitedspinal.org

National Spinal Cord Injury Association: www.spinalcord.org

For Caregivers and Families:

Family Caregiver Alliance: 1-800-445-8106 | www.caregiver.org

National Alliance for Caregiving: www.caregiving.org

These organizations understand. They've heard stories like yours.

They won't judge. They're there to help.

I have added reference material at the back of the book in the references section. The topics are related to the story.

Prologue

I don't dive into pools anymore. I haven't in twenty years...

Beth doesn't know why. After being married for four years she's never asked, probably figured it was just a quirk of mine. Perhaps she thought it was similar to how I can't stand the smell of Fireball whiskey or how I always check the locks twice before bed. Everyone's got their things. This was one of mine.

We were on the couch, on a Tuesday night, nothing special. I'd just gotten home from the dealership. Yeah, I'm still a service writer after all these years. I never could escape the car business and Beth had the news on while she folded laundry. I wasn't really watching; I was decompressing which was my normal routine. I was letting the day drain out of me, thinking about nothing really. Until the story came on.

A young person in Chandler... Nineteen years old. They dove into a pool at a party, hitting the shallow end wrong. They were showing the backyard with the pool and that yellow caution tape around it. His parents were standing in the driveway looking like someone had scooped out everything inside them and left the shells standing there. The reporter was saying words like "cervical injury" and "paralysis" and "life-altering," and I felt something crack open in my chest that I'd kept sealed for two decades. I didn't move. I couldn't breathe as the room went sideways. "Rob?"

I heard Beth's voice, somewhere far away.

"Rob, what's wrong?"

I couldn't answer. My hands were shaking. I looked down at them like they belonged to someone else, these thick fingers that had been elbow-deep in transmissions for twenty years, and all I could see were different hands with long fingers. They were usually steady with a cigarette always looking natural there.

"Hey." Beth was next to me now, the laundry forgotten, her hand on my arm. "Talk to me. What is it?"

I looked at the TV. They'd moved on to weather. It was going to be sunny and seventy-five tomorrow, like the world hadn't just ripped open. "I knew someone," I said. My voice sounded wrong... rusty. "A long time ago."

"Someone who...?" She glanced at the TV, then back at me. "Oh, Rob."

"It was twenty years ago."

"You never told me."

"No." I rubbed my face with both hands and tried to get my breathing under control. "I never told anyone... Not really."

Beth sat back and gave me some space. That was one of the things I loved about her... she knew when to push and when to wait. Right now, she was waiting and I was grateful for it. The thing is, I'd spent twenty years not talking about Doyle. Not because I'd forgotten him... you don't forget someone like that. It was because talking about him meant going back there. To the apartment on Greenway and Tatum. To the bars, the smoke, the girls in their Rockies. To the dealership on Bell Road where we'd spent our days covered in grease and trans fluid, or in his case, clean as a whistle because trim guys don't get dirty like heavy line guys do.

I was being taken back to the pool. The party... the night I wasn't there because I was out with some girl whose name I can't even remember now. "His name was Doyle," I said. I hadn't said that name out loud in years. It felt strange in my mouth, like a word from a dead language. "Robert Doyle. We worked together. We were roommates and he was my best friend for a time."

Beth didn't say anything, she just listened. "We called each other by our last names because we were both Roberts. It was easier that way. So, he was Doyle, and I was Hanson, and that's who we were."

I stopped. The news had moved on to sports; some highlight reel I couldn't have cared less about. Twenty years ago, Doyle wouldn't have cared either. He wasn't a TV guy. People were his jam. He could charm just about anyone. He could walk into a room looking like he'd just rolled off a dirt road, all homely and skinny with that curly black hair that never knew what to do with itself. And somehow every eye would turn toward him. Every woman would lean a little closer. Every conversation would shift in his direction.

I was six feet, blonde, blue eyes, buff from lifting engines and transmissions all day. On paper, I should have been the one getting the attention. But Doyle would walk into a bar and within ten minutes he'd have three girls laughing at something he said, and I'd be standing there wondering how the hell he did it. I never figured it out. Some things can't be taught. "What happened to him?" Beth asked quietly.

And there it was... The question I'd been running from for two decades. What happened to Doyle?

Everything... Everything happened to him. The dive into the shallow end. The crack of his spine against the bottom of the pool. The months in the hospital while his body became a prison. The girlfriend who spent his money, drove his car and then left when she found out he'd never walk, move his fingers again or be the man she'd thought she was getting. The look on his face when I said I couldn't help him die, even though some part of me understood why he wanted out.

The care facility... The visits where I would watch him disappear a piece by piece... his teeth gone, his body wasting, his mind drowning in pain medication. Those hands that used to do trim work like surgery. They were precise, patient and perfect. They were just lying there uselessly while he talked about the old days. Remember when, Hanson? Remember Rockin Rodeo? Remember Rita? Remember the Two Roberts routine?

I remembered oh yes, I did... I remember all of it. And then the call where I heard they'd found him on the floor. He'd accidentally tipped himself out of his wheelchair... so they said but I thought otherwise. He landed on his stomach, and he let gravity do the work. He suffocated in some facility that smelled like disinfectants and despair. He was less than thirty years old. "Rob?" Beth's hand found mine. "You don't have to..."

"No." I squeezed her fingers. "I think I do. I think I've needed to for a long time."

My grandmother, she'd said something to me after Doyle died. I was in a bad place then, darker than I'd ever been, and she could see it. Mind the grief, she told me. It can take you too. So, I'd boxed it up and put it away. I never found out where they buried him because I knew if I stood at that grave, I would have been even more messed up...

But boxes don't stay sealed forever. The tape peels and the cardboard rots. And sometimes a news story about an unfortunate child in Chandler tears the whole thing open and suddenly you're twenty-five again. Standing in a parking lot at the end of a shift, watching your best friend lean against his dirty Dodge with a cigarette between his fingers. Neither of us knowing that in six months he'd dive into the shallow end of a pool and everything would end.

"I met him at a dealership on Bell Road," I said. "It was a Ford Lincoln dealership. Twenty years ago, a little more. He was the new trim guy, and I was in heavy line, ya know the engines ... Along with transmissions... the dirty stuff. We were both named Robert, so we went by last names."

Beth nodded, waiting. "He was... there was nobody like him, Beth. He walked into a room and people just... they wanted to be near him. He wasn't good-looking, not really. But he had this thing. This light... And when you stood next to him, some of it hit you too."

I told her about the apartment at Greenway and Tatum. It was a ground floor with two bedrooms. It had a large living room where Doyle's mess would spread like a virus no matter how much I cleaned. I told her about his bathroom that was so bad the girls would ask to use mine, and how my toilet seat was getting more action than I was. She laughed at that, and I was grateful for it... grateful that there were still parts of this story that could make someone laugh.

I told her about the bars... Rockin Rodeo in Tempe, Lucky's near Grand Ave, Harold's up in Cave Creek. Longnecks and Jim Beam, what Doyle called American muscle juice. The smoke so thick you couldn't see across the room, and you'd wake up the next day smelling like an ashtray, your clothes, your hair, everything. The girls in their Rockies... jeans without back pockets. They were all done up with their boots, hats and long hair flowing. I was hooked before I finished my first beer.

I told her about the two Roberts routine. How Doyle would walk up to a group of girls, introduce himself as Robert, then wave me over and say,

"This is my buddy, his name's Robert too." They'd never believe it until we pulled out our IDs, and by then we were already in... already picking out which one we wanted to dance with before they even realized what had happened.

I told her about the country boy who taught this city kid how to live. About the craftsman whose hands could do things with trim work that made the other techs stop and watch. About a friend who never made me feel small even though I was always in his shadow. I didn't mind, because shadows don't complain when the light is that good. And then I told her about the pool.

The party neither of us was supposed to be at. The night I wasn't there because I'd gone out with some girl. The dive into the shallow end. The sound... or what I imagine the sound was, because I wasn't there... I wasn't there; I've spent twenty years living with the guilt of not being there.

C4, they called it. A complete spinal cord injury at the fourth cervical vertebra. Paralysis from the shoulders down. No movement in his hands, his arms, his legs. A man defined by what his hands could do, and suddenly they couldn't do anything. A man who lived for people, for connection, for the touch of a woman's hand on his arm, trapped in a body that couldn't feel, couldn't reach, couldn't hold.

A fate worse than death. That's what it was, he knew it and I knew it. His mother the nurse knew it even though she kept talking about advances in medicine, holding onto hope that was just a slower way of falling.

I skimmed over it while telling Beth about Tara, the girlfriend who left. The garage at his parents' house, his stepfather Steve who didn't want him there. The gun conversation along with Amy, the caretaker who stole his stuff for heroin and passed out while he lay there hungry and needing his medication. The facility.... The end.

After the quick version, the house was quiet. The TV had gone to some late-night show, the volume too low to hear. Beth hadn't said anything in a long time. She just held my hand and let me talk. "I never found out where they buried him," I said. "I couldn't. If I'd stood at that grave..." I shook my head. "My grandmother was right. The grief would have done a number on me too."

Beth wiped her eyes with her free hand. "Twenty years you've carried this."

"Yeah."

"Why didn't you ever tell me?"

I thought about it. Really thought. "Because saying it out loud makes it real. And as long as I didn't say it, I could pretend it was just a bad dream. Something that happened to someone else, a long time ago."

"But it happened to you."

"It happened to him. I just had to watch."

She was quiet for a moment. Then... "Is that why you don't dive into pools?"

I almost laughed. Almost. "I really haven't been in a pool since it happened. I kinda wade in but I don’t go in all the way. Every time I see one, I see it... The shallow end. The tile at the bottom. The moment everything changed."

Beth leaned into me, her head on my shoulder. "I'm sorry, Rob. I'm so sorry."

"Me too."

We sat there for a while, not talking. Outside, the neighborhood was quiet. It was a normal Tuesday night in a normal suburb, and somewhere a nineteen-year-old kid was lying in a hospital bed learning that his life was never going to be what he thought it would be. Mind the grief. It can take you too. But maybe it doesn't have to. Maybe talking about it, finally, after twenty years... maybe that's how you survive. You find someone who'll listen, someone who'll hold your hand in the dark, and you say the name out loud. Doyle.

Robert Doyle. Twenty-four when he dove into that pool and still under thirty when he found his way out. One of the best friends I ever had, and I watched him lose everything... his girl, his hands, his dignity, his life. I don't dive into pools anymore. Now you know why. Beth wanted to hear the whole story, with all the details... “Start at the beginning...” she said. It wasn’t for her. She did it for me, so I could process it...

Chapter One – The Dealership

A dealership shop has a rhythm. You learn it or you wash out. I'd been at the Ford Lincoln one on Bell Road long enough to know the beat by heart.

Six in the morning, the bay doors go up. By then the coffee was already burnt in the break room. It's been sitting there since whoever opened. The fluorescent lights buzz overhead, that particular hum you stop hearing after a while but never really forget. The smell hits you before anything else... oil, grease, brake cleaner, and something underneath all of it that's just *cars*. Metal, rubber and the accumulated sweat of a hundred guys who came before you.

Everything was about beating flat rate. How many hours you could flag, how fast you could turn a job. If the book says a transmission swap takes six hours? You do it in four and a half, you just made six hours' pay for four and a half hours' work. That was the game and everyone was playing it. Everyone was keeping score, even if they pretended, they weren't.

You'd hear guys bragging at lunch. Forty hours flagged in a thirty-five-hour week. Fifty if it was a good one. The service writers would throw jobs on the board and techs would practically fight over them. The gravy jobs, the ones that paid well and went fast. Nobody wanted the comebacks, the warranty work, the stuff that ate up time and paid pennies. You learned to read the board like a stock ticker. You learned to move fast when something good came up.

Some guys cheated the system. They cut corners, did half the work and hoped nobody would notice. They'd get caught eventually. The word always gets around. Customer comebacks with the same problem, and suddenly everyone knows who touched it last. Your reputation was everything in a shop like that. Once you lost it, you didn't get it back.

I played it straight. Maybe that's why I never flagged the most hours or ever made the most money. But I slept fine at night, and when a car left my bay, it stayed fixed. That counted for something.

I was twenty-five that year, I was a heavy line and transmissions tech. The dirty work. The kind of jobs that left you looking like you'd crawled through an engine block by the end of the day. Grease under your fingernails that wouldn't come out no matter how much Gojo you used. Trans fluid in your hair, on your arms, sometimes in places you didn't want to think about. I was good at it... Strong enough to muscle out the hard stuff, patient enough to not break things that would cost me money. I had my bay, my tools and my routine.

There was this old guy named Earl. He'd been there forever, probably since the dealership opened. His gray hair, bad back, hands like leather gloves showed wisdom. He could out-flag me on his worst day, and he made sure I knew it. We had words more than once. I started calling him Pops just to get under his skin. "Call me that again, kid."

"Whatever you say, Pops."

He'd flip me off and go back to work. The next day would be the same thing. We'd compete for jobs, try to beat each other's times, talk trash across the shop floor. Some of the other guys thought we hated each other. We didn't... It was just how we communicated. Two guys who respected each other enough to give no quarter. He pushed me to be better, even if he'd never admit that was what he was doing. And I kept him on his toes, reminded him that the young guys were coming up fast.

"You're slowing down, Pops. I'm gonna catch you."

"The day you catch me is the day I retire, kid. And I ain't retiring."

He never did catch me calling him Earl. To me, he was always Pops and still is, in my memory.

You couldn't be soft in a shop like that. The guys would test you from day one. They'd add extra parts to your bolts tray when you weren't looking, so you'd think you missed something and waste an hour tearing apart work you'd already done. They'd leave the caps barely on fluid bottles, so they'd spill when you picked them up. They'd hide your ten-millimeter socket, which was funny exactly zero times but happened at least once a week. They'd tell the new service writer you were the guy to ask about the nonexistent part for a made-up repair, just to watch you try to explain what a "muffler bearing" was.

Stupid stuff, but it added up. If you couldn't take it, if you complained or got angry, they'd do it more. The only way out was through. You had to give it back, worse than you got. You had to laugh when they got you and plot your revenge for later. That's how you earned respect.

I earned mine by short-sheeting Pops' toolbox so the drawers wouldn't close right. He spent half a morning trying to figure out what was wrong before he found the playing cards I'd slipped into the tracks. He didn't say anything. Just looked at me across the shop, nodded once, and went back to work. That's when I knew I was in.

I had respect after that. Not the most, not the least but just enough. They knew me as steady and reliable. The kind of guy who showed up, did the work, didn't cause problems but could take a joke as well as dish one out. There's value in that, even if it doesn't make you memorable. Then the new guy showed up.

Word travels fast in a shop. He was a new hire coming in, trim work. Another Robert, someone said. Great... That won't be confusing.

I didn't think much of it. Trim guys came and went. It wasn't the hardest work... interiors, dashboards, headliners, the stuff that made a car look good but didn't require you to bench-press a transmission. It was a different world from mine. We'd nod at each other, maybe grab the same pot of burnt coffee, but that was usually it.

I was under a Lincoln Town Car when he walked in. I saw his boots first. They were cowboy boots, worn but clean. Not what most guys wore in the shop. I slid out, wiped my hands on a rag that was already more grease than cloth, and got my first look at Robert Doyle.

He wasn't much to look at. Tall, too thin, curly black hair that didn't know what to do with itself. He had a face like a country road including all the angles and weather. Homely, if I'm being honest, and I always am. The kind of face you'd pass on the street and never remember.

But he walked like he owned the place before he'd ever set foot in it. That was the thing about Doyle. The thing I'd spend the next year trying to figure out and never really would. He didn't look like anything special. But something about the way he carried himself made you want to look twice. It made you want to know what he knew that you didn't.

The service manager was showing him around, pointing out the bays, the parts counter and the break room. Doyle nodded along, but his eyes were already taking in everything else... the techs, the cars and the rhythm of the place. He was reading the room before he'd even been introduced. Then he saw me watching...

He didn't look away. Most new guys would, especially getting caught staring at someone covered in transmission fluid who looked like they'd been working since dawn, but Doyle just nodded. It was easy like we already knew each other. I nodded back and that was it. That was the whole first meeting. Two guys nodding at each other across a shop floor but something about it stuck.

The service manager brought him over later that morning. I was between jobs, cleaning up, trying to get some of the grime off before it became permanent. "This is Robert. He's the new trim guy. Robert, this is Robert. Heavy line and Auto Trans."

"Two Roberts," Doyle said. That grin, the first time I saw it. "That's going to get confusing."

"Usually does," I said.

The service manager wandered off. He had actual work to do, and he left us standing there in an awkward moment. He could've ended it with a handshake and nothing else. "So, what do we do about the name thing?" Doyle asked.

"Last names," I said. "Easier that way."

"Works for me." He stuck out his hand. "Doyle."

I took it. He had a good grip, firm but not trying to prove anything. I responded with my last name… "Hanson."

And that's who we were from then on. I watched him work that first week. I couldn't help it. My bay was positioned so I could see the trim area if I looked up from what I was doing, and I found myself looking up a lot. Trim isn't my thing. I'm a transmission guy, heavy line. I like the heavy stuff, the mechanical puzzles, the satisfaction of dropping something that weighs three hundred pounds into place and having it work. But I know skill when I see it.

Doyle's hands moved like they were having a conversation with the car. He was precise and patient. He'd pull a dashboard apart in half the time it took most guys, and when he put it back together, you couldn't tell it had ever been touched. No squeaks, rattles or gaps. It was perfect.

The kind of hands that could fix anything. There was this one job, second or third day. Some electrical issue in a Town Car, one of those nightmare problems that make techs want to quit the business. The customer said the lights flickered sometimes. Sometimes... That was the problem. Intermittent electrical faults are the worst. The short could be anywhere in a hundred feet of wiring harness, and if you couldn't make it happen on demand, you were just guessing.

Richard, our master tech, had been on it for two days. Richard was the guy you went to when nobody else could figure it out. Thirty years of experience, he knew more about cars than the engineers who designed them. If Richard was stumped, it meant the job was a nightmare. He was ready to tell the service writer to send it somewhere else, take the hit to his pride rather than waste another day.

Doyle walked over during lunch, when Richard had stepped away. I watched him from my bay, curious. He opened the door, sat in the driver's seat, and just... looked. He didn't touch anything at first. He just sat there, studying the dash, the door panels and the headliner. Then he started tracing wires with his fingers, following them back from the lights to the harness, to the junction boxes.

Twenty minutes later, he'd found it. A pinched wire behind the kick panel, where someone had done a stereo install years ago and hadn't bothered to secure it properly. Every time the driver shifted their left foot a certain way, the wire would make contact with the metal bracket and short out.

Richard came back from lunch and Doyle showed him. I expected Richard to be pissed. Two days of his time, and the new kid finds it in twenty minutes. But Richard just looked at the wire, looked at Doyle, and nodded. "How'd you know to look there?"

Doyle shrugged. "Just followed the path. Electricity wants to go to ground. You follow where it wants to go, eventually you find where it's going wrong."

"You've done this before."

"A time or two... I grew up working on my grandpa's trucks. Old wiring, always shorting out. You learn to trace it before you learn to walk."

After that, any time there was an electrical gremlin, they'd call Doyle. It didn't matter that he was the trim guy, or that he'd been there a week. He could find a short in a wiring harness like a bloodhound tracking a scent faster than guys with twenty years of experience. It torqued some of them. Not Richard, though. Richard just started asking Doyle questions, picking his brain, treating him like a technician instead of a new hire. That was rare. Richard didn't treat anybody like a technician.

But that was Doyle. He made everything look easy. He made people forget that they were supposed to resent him.

And at the end of the day, I looked like I'd lost a fight with a transmission. I had grease up to my elbows, trans fluid in places I didn't want to think about, but Doyle was clean as a whistle. The dirtiest he got was crawling under a dashboard or into a trunk. He'd clock out looking like he was ready to go meet a girl. Probably because he was.

On paper, I should've been the one getting the attention. I was six foot, blonde, blue eyes, buff from lifting engines and transmissions all day. I wasn't bad-looking. I'm still not, if you ask my wife, though she might be biased.

Doyle was tall but skinny, that homely face, hair that never cooperated no matter what he did to it. If you put us side by side anyone would've picked me as the one who'd do better with women, better at parties, better at anything that required making an impression. They'd have been dead wrong.

I saw it that first week. Doyle was talking to one of the service writers. Her name was Amanda, and she was the kind of pretty that made guys stupid. Young, blonde, knew exactly what she looked like and used it to her advantage. Every tech in the shop had tried at some point. Some had tried multiple times. She shut them all down with a smile that said *nice try, keep dreaming.* After a while, the guys just stopped trying. She was off-limits, a lost cause, the one you looked at but didn't bother approaching.

Doyle walked up to her counter to drop off some paperwork and within five minutes she was laughing. Actually laughing, not the polite kind she gave customers while leaning forward on the counter. She was twirling her pen between her fingers. Touching her hair. All the things that meant something was working. I watched from across the shop, hands frozen on a wrench, trying to figure out what the hell I was seeing.

They talked for ten minutes.... Then fifteen. She wasn't even pretending to do work while she was focused on him, like he was the only person in the building. At one point she wrote something down and slid it across the counter. I couldn't see what it was from where I stood, but I could guess.

Doyle took the paper, tucked it in his pocket without looking at it, said something that made her laugh again, and walked away. It was casual. Like he hadn't just done the impossible.

How does a guy who looks like that command attention like this? I asked Pops about it later. He'd been watching too. "Kid's got something," Pops said. "Can't explain it. Either you have it or you don't."

"I don't have it."

"No." He didn't sugarcoat it. "You don't. But that's okay. Most people don't."

He wasn't doing anything special. He wasn't running lines or trying too hard. He was just *talking*. Being himself and somehow that was enough. Somehow that was more than enough. He'd walk into a room and people turned around. I'd walk into a room and people made space for me to get to the bar. That was the difference. That was always the difference.

By the end of the first week, I was heading out to the parking lot when I saw him leaning against his truck. It was a Dodge in the Ford dealership parking lot. "Nice truck," I said, and I meant it to be sarcastic, but it came out more curious. Doyle just grinned. "She runs good."

"You're a Dodge guy working at a Ford dealership?"

He shrugged, pulled a cigarette from his pocket and lit it. That easy way he had with everything, like nothing was worth getting worked up about. "Money's green, Hanson."

I laughed. I couldn't help it. "Besides," he said, exhaling smoke, "you seen what Honda's doing with those new racers? That's the future right there. Import tuners. People are sleeping on it, but they won't be for long."

"You follow that stuff?"

"I follow everything. Cars are cars. It doesn't matter what badge is on the front."

I looked at his Dodge again. Really looked at it this time. It was so dirty. Not dirty like mine got dirty, not grease and fluid, but *dirty* dirty. Dirt on the floorboards, what looked like old hay, like he'd been hauling something from a ranch. "What's all that?" I pointed at the cab. "Is that hay?"

"It adds character."

"It needs to be acquainted with a power washer at minimum."

He laughed in that laugh I'd come to know well, friendly and warm, like you'd just said the funniest thing he'd heard all day. "You sound like my mother."

"Your mother sounds smart."

He spotted my ride then. The Mustang. 5.0, hatchback, mechanic special. I'd picked it up cheap and put more work into it than I should've, but it ran like a dream and sounded even better. "That you?" he asked.

"Yeah."

He walked over, checking it out. Nodded at the engine, the body, the wheels. Then he stopped. Looked through the hatchback glass at the back. "What the hell is that?"

He was looking at the chain. I'd wrapped it around the subwoofers in the back, padlocked it to the frame. "Security system."

"It's a chain."

"Ain't nobody stealing my tunes without some extra effort."

He stared at me. Then that laugh again, louder this time, echoing across the parking lot. A couple of guys heading to their cars looked over. "A chain," he said, shaking his head. "Around your subwoofers."

"You got a problem with that?"

"No, man. No problem." He was still laughing, wiping his eyes. "I just... a chain. That's the most Hanson thing I've ever heard, and I've known you a week."

"You're one to talk. You've got hay in your truck."

"That's character."

"And this is security."

We stood there in the parking lot, the Arizona sun beating down, giving each other shit like we'd been doing it for years. Like we hadn't just met. "You want to grab a beer?" he asked. "There's a place down the road."

I should've said no. I was tired, covered in grime, wanted nothing more than a shower and my couch. But something made me say yes. Maybe it was curiosity. Maybe it was the way he asked, like it was the most natural thing in the world. Like we were already friends and just hadn't gotten around to acting like it yet. "Yeah, alright."

"Follow me." He climbed into his dirty Dodge, hay and all. "Try to keep up, Hanson."

"In that thing? I'll be waiting at the bar for you."

He flipped me off and started the engine. The dive bar was a few miles down the road. It was dark with sticky floors and the pool table had a rip in the felt along with the jukebox that only worked half the time. The kind of place where nobody asked questions and everyone minded their own business. Perfect for mechanics who wanted to wash the day off with cheap beer.

We grabbed a booth in the back. Doyle ordered us a pitcher and two shots of Jim Beam without asking what I wanted. I didn't complain. The whiskey burned going down and the beer was cold, and after a day of transmissions and trans fluid, that was exactly what I needed.

We didn't talk about work. That surprised me. Most guys, the first time you got a drink with them, they'd rehash the day. The jobs, the customers, the service writers, the other techs. Shop talk, because that's all we had in common.

Doyle talked about other things. Where he grew up... Country, out past Scottsdale, his grandparents' place with the horses and the tractors. His mom, the nurse who worried too much. His stepdad Steve, who he didn't say much about except that he was "just Steve." The bars he liked, places I'd never heard of with names like Rockin Rodeo and Harold's. The girls he'd met... stories that made me laugh and wonder if he was exaggerating but it felt like he probably wasn't.

He asked about me too. Where I was from. How I ended up at the dealership. What I did when I wasn't working. I didn't have answers as interesting as his. I was a California kid, who moved to Arizona because the work was here. I spent my off time watching TV and drinking beer alone in my apartment. Nothing worth telling stories about. "We gotta fix that," he said.

"Fix what?"

"You. The way you live." He poured another beer from the pitcher. "You work hard, Hanson. I can see that. But what's the point if you're not enjoying the rest of it?"

I didn't have an answer for that. "Tell you what," he said. "Stick with me. I'll show you how it's done."

I laughed. "How what's done?"

"Everything." That grin. "Life, Hanson. The whole thing. You're doing it wrong, and I'm gonna help you do it right."

I should have rolled my eyes. Should have told him thanks but no thanks, I was fine the way I was. But something about the way he said it made me think maybe he was right. Maybe I was doing it wrong. Maybe there was more to this than transmissions, TV and falling asleep on the couch.

Maybe this guy with hay in his truck and a face like a country road knew something I didn't. "Alright," I said. "Show me."

"That's what I like to hear." He raised his beer. "To the two Roberts."

"To the two Roberts."

We clinked glasses. Drank. And something shifted, even if I didn't recognize it at the time. A door opening that I hadn't known was there. I didn't know it then. How could I?

I just knew that this guy... this skinny, homely, magnetic guy with hay in his truck and a laugh that made you want to be in on the joke was someone worth knowing. "See you tomorrow, Hanson," he'd said at the bar that night, finishing his beer.

"See you tomorrow, Doyle."

That was the start of everything. I just didn't know it yet. You never do.

Chapter Two - Roommates

It happened fast, the way things did with Doyle. We'd been working together about three months, grabbing beers after shift most Fridays, getting to know each other in that way guys do... through bullshit and silence and the occasional real conversation. I wouldn't have called us best friends yet, but we were something. Something more than coworkers. Then his roommate bailed.

We were in the parking lot, after the end of a Thursday shift, and Doyle was leaning against his Dodge with a cigarette going, same as always. But something was off. He wasn't joking around. He wasn't giving me shit about the chain on my subwoofers or the way I'd taken too long on a transmission rebuild that day. "What's eating you?" I asked.

He took a drag, exhaled toward the Arizona sky. "My roommate's bailing. The lease is up at the end of the month."

"That sucks."

"Yeah." Another drag. "I guess the guy got a girl pregnant. He's moving in with her. I can't really blame him, but the timing's shit."

I thought about my own situation. I was in a studio apartment on the other side of town. It was cramped with loud neighbors along with a landlord who thought fixing things was optional. I'd been thinking about moving anyway, just hadn't gotten around to it. "I've been looking for something bigger," I said. I didn't plan on saying it. It just came out.

Doyle looked at me. "Yeah?"

"Yeah. My place is a shithole."

"Mine's not bad. But I can't swing the rent alone."

We stood there, both of us doing the math. Two incomes with a split rent and someone you could actually stand living with.

"You in?" Doyle asked.

I should've thought about it. I should've asked about the lease terms, the neighborhood, whether he left dishes in the sink. But that wasn't how it worked with Doyle. Things just made sense with him. Decisions that would take me weeks to overthink, he'd make in seconds and somehow, they always turned out right. "I'm in."

He grinned, that grin. "Alright then. Let's go find a place."

We looked at three apartments that weekend. The first one was too small. The second one was in a neighborhood I didn't love. Nothing you could point to specifically, just a feeling. Doyle felt it too. "Let's keep looking."

The third one was on Greenway and Tatum. It was on the ground floor with two bedrooms and a living room big enough to actually live in. The carpet was old, the appliances were older, and the AC unit made a sound like it was dying slowly. But it had space and was filled with light. It had room to breathe.

The landlord was a guy named Martinez in his mid-fifties, suspicious of everyone. He had probably been burned by too many tenants who trashed his places and skipped on rent. He looked at us like we were already problems he'd have to deal with. Then Doyle went to work. "Look, man," Doyle said, all friendly confidence, leaning against the kitchen counter like he already lived there. "Two working guys. Steady jobs at the Ford dealership on Bell Road. You can call our manager if you want, he'll vouch for us. We're not gonna trash your place. We're not gonna throw parties every weekend. We just need somewhere to sleep and keep our stuff."

Martinez grunted, he wasn't convinced yet. "And between you and me," Doyle continued, lowering his voice like he was sharing a secret, "you know how hard it is to find tenants who actually pay on time? Who don't call you every five minutes because the faucet drips or the carpet's got a stain? That's not us. We're mechanics. If something breaks, we'll fix it ourselves. You won't hear from us unless the roof caves in."

I watched the landlord's face soften despite himself. That was Doyle's gift. He could make anyone like him. Even people who'd made up their minds not to. Martinez dropped the deposit by two hundred bucks, and we signed the lease that afternoon. It wasn't fancy, but it was ours.

Move-in day was brutal... July in Arizona. It was a hundred and ten degrees, maybe more. The kind of heat that hits you like a wall when you step outside, that makes you question every life choice that led you to living in a desert. The asphalt in the parking lot was soft under our boots. You could feel it giving, like it might swallow you if you stood still too long. The air shimmered off the cars, off the concrete, off everything. By nine in the morning, my shirt was soaked through. By noon, I'd stopped bothering to wipe the sweat out of my eyes.

We loaded up our vehicles... Doyle's Dodge, my Mustang and a borrowed trailer for the bigger stuff. His Dodge was a mess, as usual. Dirt on the floorboards, old hay from God knows where, fast food wrappers crammed between the seats. I made the mistake of opening the passenger door and got hit with a wall of heat and stale cigarette smoke. "When's the last time you cleaned this thing?"

"It adds character." He was already hauling a box out of the back. "You gonna help or you gonna critique my housekeeping?"

We spent the day hauling boxes and furniture up the walkway and through the front door. In and out, in and out, the AC inside barely making a dent before we'd be back in the heat again. The walkway was maybe thirty feet but it felt like a mile by the fifth trip.

Neither of us had much. A bed each, some clothes, the essentials. He had a stereo that he treated like a firstborn child. It was nicer than anything else he owned. He carried it in himself and he wouldn't let me touch it. He set it up in the living room before we'd even brought in our beds. "Priorities," he said, when I pointed that out.

"We don't have anywhere to sleep."

"But we've got music." He plugged it in, and George Strait filled the apartment. "See? Now it's home."

The TV had seen better days. The picture was washed out on one side, and you had to hit it sometimes to get the color right. But it worked good enough. Then there was the couch. I don't know where he got it. I asked once, and he said, "Don't ask questions you don't want answers to, Hanson." It was brown or maybe green. It was hard to tell, with the stains. The cushions sagged in the middle like they'd given up years ago. It smelled like cigarette smoke and something else I couldn't identify and didn't want to. "We're not keeping this," I said, standing over it in the living room. "It's comfortable."

"It's a health hazard."

"It's broken in. That's different."

I lost that argument. The couch stayed. It became a fixture and the place where everyone sat. It was where beers were spilled and never got quite cleaned up. Doyle would pass out after a long night, and I'd throw a blanket over him on my way to bed. I hated that couch but I kind of loved it too.

We cracked our first beers around sunset, sitting on that questionable couch, the AC struggling against the heat, boxes stacked around us like cardboard walls. The apartment was a mess. We were exhausted, soaked in sweat, probably dehydrated but we were home. "Not bad," Doyle said, surveying the chaos.

"It's a disaster."

"It's our disaster." He clinked his bottle against mine. "To the apartment."

"To the apartment."

Living with Doyle was an education. The man was a pig. I don't say that with judgment... okay, maybe a little judgment but mostly it's just a fact. Clothes on the floor, dishes in the sink, ashtrays overflowing onto every flat surface. He'd walk in the door after work, kick off his boots wherever they landed, and leave a trail of debris from the entrance to his bedroom like a tornado with a direct path.

The ashtrays were the worst. He'd fill one up, then start using a coffee mug. He'd fill that up and move to a beer can. By the end of the week, there'd be five or six makeshift ashtrays scattered around the living room, each one overflowing with butts and ash. The whole apartment smelled like a bar at closing time. That was just how it was back then... you could smoke anywhere, and Doyle smoked everywhere.

I was the opposite. Maybe too much the opposite. I liked things clean, organized, in their place. Growing up, my parents ran a tight ship, and I guess it stuck. Dirty dishes bothered me. Clutter bothered me. Walking into the living room to find Doyle's crap spread across every surface like he'd exploded... that really bothered me. "You live like an animal, Doyle."

"And you live like my mother. Relax, Hanson."

"There are dishes in the sink from three days ago."

"They're soaking."

"They're growing things."

He'd just laugh. That warm, friendly laugh that made it hard to stay mad at him. Then he'd go right back to being a slob, and I'd go right back to cleaning up after him, and we'd do the same dance the next day. I'd wipe down the counters; he'd leave a ring from his beer bottle. I'd take out the trash; he'd let it pile up until it was overflowing. It was like living with a force of nature... You couldn't fight it; you just had to work around it. I gave up after awhile and just got used to it...

The thing was, he wasn't dirty at work. That was the strange part. At the dealership, his tools were clean, his work area was neat, his cars were spotless when he finished with them. But the second he walked through our front door; it was like a switch flipped. Home was where he let go. Where he didn't have to try.

"You're clean at work," I said once. "Why can't you be clean here?"

He thought about it for a second, cigarette dangling from his lip. "At work, I'm getting paid. Here, I'm off the clock."

The bathroom was ground zero. His bathroom, specifically. I learned early on to keep mine clean, door closed, separate from whatever was happening in his. Because whatever was happening in his was bad. Towels on the floor, soap scum on everything, toothpaste dried on the sink like modern art. The toilet... I won't describe the toilet. Let's just say I never used it, not once, the entire time we lived together.

Every girl who came over took one look at his bathroom and asked to use mine. Almost every single one. They'd peek in, see the horror show, and turn around with this look on their face like they'd just witnessed a crime scene. "Can I use your bathroom?" they'd ask me, already knowing the answer.

"Down the hall on the left."

Doyle thought it was hilarious. "Hanson, your bathroom's getting more action than you are."

He wasn't wrong. But somehow, despite everything, it worked. He was a slob and I was wound too tight. We met somewhere in the middle or I just gave up. Probably that... You can't change a person. You either accept them or you don't. I accepted him... mess, smoke, chaos, and all.

The apartment became a gathering spot. I don't know how that happened. One day it was just me and Doyle, and the next there were people everywhere, showing up at all hours, like the place had been designated the official hangout location and nobody told me.

Doyle drew people in. That was his gift. Wherever he went, people followed. Buddies from the dealership, guys Doyle knew from somewhere... he always knew someone from somewhere. A buddy from high school. A cousin's friend. Some guy he met at a gas station once. Girls, of course. There were always girls. They'd show up in pairs, giggling, following him home from the bar like he was the Pied Piper.

They'd show up on a Friday night, and suddenly we'd have ten people in the living room, music playing, beers flowing, Doyle holding court like he'd been born to do it. Country music on that stereo of his... George Strait, Chris LeDoux, the soundtrack of his life. The smoke would get so thick you had to open the patio door wall. Everybody smoking, everybody drinking, the AC working overtime and losing the battle.

He'd start building these towers out of empty beer cans, stacking them carefully, one on top of another, seeing how high he could get them before the whole thing collapsed. It became a thing, a ritual. People would gather around, watching, placing bets on when it would fall. By midnight, he'd have a tower going halfway to the ceiling, balancing cans with the precision of a surgeon. Every time he added another one, he'd get this look on his face. That grin. That laugh. Like he was getting away with something. He probably was.

When the tower finally fell... and it always fell, usually because someone bumped the coffee table or laughed too hard, the whole room would erupt. Doyle never got mad or frustrated. He'd just start stacking again, cigarette in one hand, beer in the other, like the collapse was part of the fun. Maybe it was...

I'd watch from the edge of the room, beer in hand, taking it all in. I wasn't the life of the party. That wasn't my role. My role was to be there, in the orbit, enjoying the show. And it was a show. Doyle could talk to anyone about anything and make them feel like the most interesting person in the room. He had that gift, like whatever they had to say was exactly what he'd been waiting to hear. People opened up to him and told him things. Strangers became friends in the time it took to finish a beer.

Me, I had to work for that. Every conversation, every connection, felt like effort. With Doyle, it was effortless. He didn't need entertainment. He was the entertainment. The mornings after those parties were something else. I'd wake up to bodies on the couch, on the floor, people

I half-recognized from the night before. The apartment would smell like stale beer and cigarettes, empties everywhere, the beer can tower collapsed in a pile by the TV. I'd step over sleeping strangers to make coffee, and Doyle would eventually emerge from his room, hair sticking up, grinning like nothing had happened. "Hell of a night," he'd say.

"There are people in our living room."

"They'll leave eventually."

One night, I woke up to what looked like a supermodel in her underwear stepping out of my bathroom. She stopped dead when she saw me standing in the hallway, half-asleep and confused. "Oh God. Sorry. Robert said I could use..."

"It's fine." I was too tired to be embarrassed. "Coffee?"

She nodded, wrapped a towel around herself, and sat at the kitchen table like this was normal. For that apartment, it was. Doyle wandered out a few minutes later, kissed her on the forehead, poured himself a cup like it was any other morning. I didn't mind... it was like he had stated... My toilet seat was getting more ass than me.

The best nights were the quiet ones. No visitors or parties. Just me and Doyle, both of us wiped from work, sprawled on the couch with the TV on and beers in hand. I'd flip through channels, looking for something to watch. He'd ignore whatever I landed on and start talking instead.

Doyle wasn't a TV guy or a sports guy either. He didn't care about the game or need the background noise that most people use to fill silence. I'd land on a football game, and he'd talk right through it. I'd find a movie, and he'd ask me questions about my life instead of watching. People were his thing... Even when it was just the two of us, he'd rather talk than watch anything. At first, that threw me off. I was used to roommates who planted themselves in front of the screen and didn't move until bedtime. Doyle was different. He wanted to know things. About me, about my life, about what made me tick. "You got family around here?" he asked one night, out of nowhere.

"Some. My folks are in California. I moved here for work."

"You close with them?"

"Close enough. I talk to my mom every few weeks. Dad and I... we're fine. Not much to say, but we're fine."

He nodded, lit a cigarette, watched the smoke curl toward the ceiling. "My mom's in Scottsdale. Stepdad too."

"You close with them?"

"My mom, yeah. She's a nurse. Good woman. She worries too much, but that's what moms do." He paused, took a drag. "Steve... Steve's just Steve."

I didn't push. You learn to read when someone's done talking about something, and Doyle was done talking about Steve. I'd learn more later... about the coldness there, the distance, the way Doyle never quite felt welcome in his own mother's house after she remarried. But that night, he just let it sit. We talked for hours. About nothing, really and somehow everything. The jobs we'd had, the places we'd been, the girls who got away and the ones we were glad did. He told me about growing up country, about the horses his grandparents kept, about learning to ride before he learned to drive. "You ever ride a bull?" I asked.

He laughed, shook his head. "Hell no. Horses, broncos when I was younger, sure. But bulls?" He took a drag. "I'm not that stupid, Hanson.

That's for other people. There's a line between brave and dumb, and I try to stay on the right side of it."

I filed that away. I didn't know it would matter later. He talked about the bars he loved, the country scene, the girls in their Rockies and boots. He talked about his grandparents' place out in the country, how he'd spend summers there as a kid, how that was where he learned what mattered and what didn't. I told him about the city, about feeling out of place in Arizona sometimes, about wondering if I'd ever figure out what I was supposed to do with my life. I told him about the shop, about the competition with Pops, about how I was always trying to prove something and never knew what. "You think too much," he said.

"You don't think enough."

"Maybe... But which one of us is happier right now?"

I didn't have an answer for that. "You're doing it," he said, after a while.

"Doing what?"

"Living... This." He gestured at the apartment, the couch, the beer in his hand. "This is it, Hanson. Right now. You're not supposed to figure it out. You're just supposed to do it."

I didn't know what to say to that. So, I didn't say anything. I just sat there, in the comfortable silence, and let it be enough. That was the night I realized he wasn't just a roommate. He was the closest thing I had to a brother. Doyle could charm just about anyone. But that night, he wasn't charming me. He was just being real. No audience, no performance, just two guys on a shitty couch in a smoke-filled apartment, trying to figure out life. That's when I knew.

Looking back, those were some of the best months of my life. I didn't know it then. You never do. The apartment at Greenway and Tatum with that questionable couch. The constant battle between his mess and my cleaning. The nights with too many people and the nights with just us. The smoke and the laughter and the sense that we had all the time in the world. We were young. We were broke most of the time, living paycheck to paycheck, spending whatever was left on beer, bars and gas money. We didn't have plans beyond the next weekend. We didn't think about the future much... retirement, families, careers. That was all abstract, far away and something for other people to worry about. We were too busy living to think about where it was all going.

That was Doyle's gift, I think. He taught me how to be present. How to stop worrying about tomorrow and just be here, now, in this moment. He didn't do it with words or lectures. He did it by example. By being the most alive person, I'd ever met.

I think about it sometimes, late at night, when Beth is asleep and the house is quiet. What it felt like to be twenty-five and have a brother in the next room. Someone who'd give you shit about your subwoofer chain but have your back when it mattered. Someone who made every room brighter just by walking into it. Someone who could turn a Thursday night into an adventure and make a dump of an apartment feel like the center of the universe.

The apartment is still there. Obviously with different tenants now, different lives playing out in those rooms. They don't know what happened there. They don't know about the two Roberts who lived there once, who built something without knowing what it was or how much it would cost to lose it. They don't know about the parties, the beer can towers, the couch that should've been condemned. They don't know that two kids became brothers in that living room, between the cigarette smoke, the country music and the late-night conversations that didn't mean anything.

Some nights, if I think about it too hard, I can still smell the cigarette smoke. I can still hear that laugh and see him on the couch, feet up, cigarette going, that grin on his face like he knew something the rest of us didn't. Maybe he did. Maybe he knew that you can't hold onto anything forever. That the good times don't last. That you've got to live while you can, because you never know when it's going to end. But then I remember what came after and I had to stop remembering for a while.

We'd been living together about two months when Doyle came home from work with that look in his eye. The one that meant he had an idea I probably wouldn't like. "You ever been to a real country bar, Hanson?"

"Can't say I have."

"Well." He grabbed his keys off the counter, flicked his cigarette into the ashtray he never emptied. "That's about to change in the near future."

Chapter Three – Country Education

The invitation came on a Thursday, at the end of shift, in the parking lot where most of our conversations happened. Doyle was leaning against his Dodge with a cigarette going, watching the sun drop behind the strip malls along Bell Road. I was heading to my Mustang, ready to go home and do nothing, same as every other Thursday. "What are you doing tomorrow night?" he asked.

I shrugged. "Nothing. TV maybe. There's a game on."

He shook his head like I'd said something pitiful. "You ever been to a real country bar, Hanson?"

I had to admit I hadn't. I'd been to bars, sure. Sports bars, dive bars, the kind of places where you drink cheap beer and watch whatever game is on. But a country bar? That wasn't my world. "You know I haven't."

"As I said then... That's about to change." He flicked ash off his cigarette and grinned. "We leave at eight."

I started to ask questions, but he was already climbing into the Dodge. The engine rumbled to life and he pulled out of the lot, one hand on the wheel, the other holding that cigarette out the window. I stood there wondering what I'd just agreed to.

Friday night I got ready the way I always got ready. Jeans, a decent shirt, sneakers that weren't too beat up. I figured I looked fine. I was wrong.

Doyle knocked and entered my room. He took one look at me and started laughing. Not mocking, just... amused. Like I'd shown up to a wedding in swim trunks. "You can't wear that."

"What's wrong with it?"

He walked past me into the apartment and started going through my closet. He rejected everything. The shoes were wrong. The shirt was wrong. The jeans were ok and he added something strange... "These jeans have back pockets," he said, holding them up like evidence.

"So?"

"So... the girls at the country bar wear Rockies. Jeans without back pockets. You'll understand when you see them. Trust me."

I didn't understand. I didn't even know what he was talking about but I trusted him, and I let him put together an outfit from what little I had that he deemed acceptable. A button-down shirt, old boots I'd forgotten I owned. When I looked in the mirror, I felt like I was wearing a costume. "You look almost passable," he said. "Let's go."

We took his Dodge. The thing was a mess, same as always with empty cigarette packs wedged between the seats. I made the mistake of looking down at my feet and seeing something I couldn't identify. My look must have said it all...

He just laughed and turned up the radio. Country music, of course. Garth Brooks singing about something lost and something found. Doyle's hand was out the window, cigarette between his fingers, and he drove like a man who knew exactly where he was going.

On the way, he coached me. How to act in a country bar. Be polite... Tip well. Don't start anything you can't finish along with how to talk to country girls. Be genuine and don't try too hard. Ask questions and actually listen to the answers. What to expect when we got there. The music would be loud. The smoke would be thick. The dancing would be something I'd never seen before.

"It's two-step mostly," he said. "You don't know how to two-step."

"I can learn."

"We'll see."

He talked about that bar like he was taking me to church. Like it was something sacred, something that mattered. I didn't get it yet. But I would.

We pulled into the parking lot of Rockin Rodeo in Tempe and I knew immediately that I was out of my depth. There were trucks everywhere. Big trucks, lifted trucks, trucks with flags and NRA stickers. Neon signs glowing in the Arizona night. You could hear the music from outside, bass thumping through the walls, and people were spilling out the front door, smoking, laughing and living.

Doyle was already nodding at people. He knew everyone, or at least everyone seemed to know him. A guy in a cowboy hat slapped his shoulder as we walked past. A girl with long blonde hair called his name and waved. He raised a hand, grinned and kept walking.

We pushed through the front door and I got hit with it all at once. The smoke was thick enough to taste. A gray haze that hung in the air, catching the neon lights, making everything look dreamlike. The music was loud with some guy singing about a honky-tonk and a broken heart. The crowd was packed tight with cowboy hats, boots and belt buckles the size of my fist.

And then I saw the Rockies... Doyle had tried to explain, but he was right. You had to see them to understand. Girls in jeans so tight they looked painted on, and those jeans had no back pockets. Just smooth denim curving over everything. The way they fit. The way those girls moved. I stood there with my mouth probably hanging open.

They were all knockouts to me. Every single one of them. They were done up with their boots, their cowboy hats and their long hair flowing down their backs. Some had their hair curled, some straight, some tucked behind their ears to show off dangly earrings. They wore tank tops and denim jackets and smiles that could stop your heart.

I was hooked before I finished my first beer or was it before I even had a beer. I can't recall but standing in that doorway, watching those girls move through the smoke and the neon, I understood why Doyle had brought me here. "Close your mouth, Hanson," Doyle said, clapping me on the back. "You look like a virgin at his first rodeo."

"Isn't that what I am?"

"Tonight, it is. Tomorrow you'll know better."

He steered me through the crowd to the bar. People parted for him. Not like he was pushing through, but like they just naturally made room. He had that effect.

We grabbed spots at the bar and Doyle ordered for both of us. Two longnecks and two Jim Beams. "What's the whiskey for?" I asked.

"American muscle juice, Hanson. You can't two-step on beer alone."

I didn't argue. I knocked back the whiskey and felt it burn down to my stomach, then chased it with cold beer. The combination hit different than what I was used to. There was something about the mix of cold beer and warm whiskey that made the room feel friendlier. It made the music sound better and made those girls in their Rockies look even more like something out of a dream.

The bartender was a big guy with a handlebar mustache and tattoos running up both arms. His forearms were thick as tree trunks and covered in faded ink. Navy anchors along with a mermaid on one side. Some kind of skull on the other. He moved with the efficiency of a man who'd been pouring drinks since before I was born. Doyle knew him. Of course he did. "Danny, this is Hanson. He works with me at the dealership."

Danny looked at me. His eyes were small and sharp, like he was sizing me up and filing the information away for later. Then he nodded, he didn't smile and went back to pouring drinks. That was apparently all the introduction I needed. In Danny's world, Doyle's word was enough.

I turned around and watched the room while Doyle lit another cigarette. The dance floor was packed. There were couples moving in that two-step he'd mentioned, spinning and stepping, somehow never crashing into each other. It looked choreographed but it wasn't. It was just... natural. Like they'd all been doing it since birth.

Doyle leaned close so I could hear him over the music. "See that girl by the pool table? She's here with someone. Don't even look."

"How can you tell?"

"Body language. She's facing the door, not the room. She's waiting for someone, not looking."

I watched and he was right. A guy came through the door a minute later and she lit up like Christmas. She went straight to him, kissed him, pulled him toward the bar.

"Now that one," Doyle said, nodding toward a brunette near the dance floor, "she's been looking over here since we sat down. Give it ten minutes."

It was like he was reading a language I couldn't see. The room was just a room to me with people, smoke and noise. To him it was a map with hidden trails that held signs and destinations marked clearly. "The bartender's brother owns the place," he added. "Tip him good and he'll remember you."

I slid an extra five across the bar when Danny brought our second round. He nodded and almost smiled.

Three whiskeys in, Doyle stubbed out his cigarette and finished his beer in one long pull. He set the bottle down and looked at me. "Watch and learn, Hanson."

He pushed off from the bar and walked toward a group of girls near the edge of the dance floor. There were three of them, all beautiful, all intimidating. The kind of girls I would have stared at from across the room and never approached.

Doyle walked up like he owned the place. Not aggressive, not pushy, just... confident. Like approaching them was the most natural thing in the world. I couldn't hear what he said over the music, but I saw the effect. One of them laughed almost immediately. Another leaned in to hear him better. The third one was smiling before he finished his first sentence.

I watched from the bar, nursing my beer, feeling like I was taking notes for a class I'd never pass. He had his hand on one girl's arm within two minutes. The casual touch that said they were connected now. All three of them were focused on him, leaning in, laughing at things he said. He told a story with his hands, acting something out, and they all cracked up.

I tried to figure out what he was saying. I was trying to read his lips and catch some hint of the magic words that made women melt like that. But there was nothing I could identify. No trick, no gimmick or secret phrase. It was just him. The way he stood. The way he smiled. The way he made each of them feel like she was the only person in the room, even while he was talking to all three.

The song changed. It was something faster, with a fiddle cutting through the bass. One of the girls started swaying, and without missing a beat, Doyle took her hand and spun her once. Right there at the edge of the dance floor. Just a single spin, casual as breathing. She laughed and fell back into the group, and now they were all looking at him like he was the best thing that had happened to them all week. Then he waved me over.

I almost choked on my beer. I wasn't ready. I didn't know what to do, what to say, where to put my hands. But he was waving, and the girls were looking, so I put down my bottle and walked over like a man approaching his own execution. "This is Hanson," Doyle said, throwing an arm around my shoulder. "He works with me. First time at a country bar. Be gentle with him."

They laughed. Not at me, but at the situation. One of them, a redhead with freckles and a smile that could light up a coal mine, stuck out her hand. "I'm Jenny. These are my friends, Carla and Diane."

I shook her hand and said something stupid that I don't remember. They didn't seem to mind. "He's shy," Doyle said. "But he's a good guy. Better mechanic than me, probably."

"Good with his hands huh...," Jenny said, and they all laughed again.

Just like that, I was in. Not because of anything I did. Because Doyle had vouched for me. Because the light that came off him hit me too. I stood there next to him and the conversation flowed around me. I said things when I could, laughed when everyone else did, and slowly started to relax.

That was his gift. He didn't just work a room for himself. He brought you in with him and made you look good just by standing next to you.

Later, after another round of drinks and some dancing I'd rather not describe, I was leaning against the bar again. Jenny had gone off with her friends and Doyle was talking to someone new. A blonde this time, tall and pretty in a way that seemed almost excessive.

She wasn't interested. I could tell from across the room. Arms crossed, looking past him, giving him nothing. But Doyle kept talking, kept trying.

Then she said something. I don't know what. But she turned and started to walk away.

And Doyle, three Jim Beams past his limit, called after her. "No, you look fat in those pants anyway."

I about spit out my beer. The blonde stopped, turned, looked at him like he'd lost his mind. For a second I thought there was going to be a fight. I thought some cowboy boyfriend was going to appear out of nowhere and put Doyle through a window. But Doyle just stood there with that grin on his face. That infuriating, charming, unkillable grin. And after a long moment, the blonde shook her head, maybe half-smiling despite herself, and walked away.

I grabbed his arm when he came back to the bar. "What the hell, Doyle?"

He shrugged. "She started it."

"She said no!"

"Exactly."

He lit another cigarette, ordered another whiskey, and acted like nothing had happened. That was the thing about Doyle. He couldn't let a rejection go without getting the last word in. He'd stir the pot just to watch it bubble. Not mean, exactly. Just... incapable of walking away quiet. "You're going to get us killed," I said.

"Hasn't happened yet."

Around midnight, Doyle nudged me and pointed toward the end of the bar. "That one's been looking at you."

I turned and saw her. Dark hair, pretty face, wearing jeans and a flannel shirt that shouldn't have looked as good as it did. She was watching me. Actually, watching me, not just looking in my general direction. "Go talk to her."

"I don't know what to say."

"Just be yourself. Ask her about herself. And for God's sake, listen."

"That's it?"

"That's everything."

I finished my beer for courage and walked over. My heart was pounding so hard I could feel it in my throat. I didn't know what I was doing. I'd never been good at this. But I remembered what Doyle said and I tried. "Hey."

Real smooth, Hanson. Great opener.

But she smiled. "Hey yourself."

Her name was Michelle. She worked at a bank downtown. She hated her job, but the hours were good and it paid the bills. She'd grown up in Flagstaff, moved to Phoenix for a boyfriend who turned out to be the kind of mistake you only make once. Two years of her life she'd never get back, she said, but at least she'd learned something. She came to Rockin Rodeo every few weeks because she liked the music and the atmosphere and the way people didn't take themselves too seriously. "Everyone's just here to have fun," she said. "No pretense, no games. You know exactly what you're getting."

I told her I was a mechanic and worked at a Ford dealership on Bell

Road. Heavy line, mostly transmissions. She asked what that meant and I explained it, probably going into too much detail, but she seemed genuinely interested. Or at least she was good at pretending. I told her I'd never been to a country bar before tonight. That my friend Doyle had basically dragged me here and I was glad he did. She laughed at that. "Doyle? The one working the room like he owns the place?"

I looked over. Doyle was at the other end of the bar now, talking to yet another group of girls. He caught my eye and raised his beer in a silent salute. "That's him."

"He's got a way about him," she said. "But you seem different. Quieter. More... real, maybe."

I didn't know what to say to that, so I just ordered us another round. We talked for an hour. Maybe more. The bar started clearing out around us and I barely noticed. The smoke was thinning as people left, but I could still taste it. The music had slowed down, sad songs about lost loves and long highways. Michelle told me about her sister in California and the dog she'd had as a kid along with the trip she wanted to take to Nashville someday. I told her about growing up in California, about moving to Arizona for work, about the way Doyle had started teaching me to live a little.

When last call came, she reached into her purse and pulled out a pen. She wrote her number on a napkin and slid it across the bar. "Call me sometime," she said. "If you want."

"I want."

She smiled, grabbed her jacket, and disappeared into the thinning crowd. I stood there holding that napkin like it was a winning lottery ticket. Doyle appeared at my elbow. "Not bad, Hanson. Not bad at all."

"She gave me her number."

"I saw." He clapped me on the back. "Let's get out of here before you screw it up."

The parking lot was almost empty when we stumbled out. The warm Arizona air hit us like a wall, clean after hours of smoke. I could finally breathe without tasting cigarettes. My clothes reeked. My hair reeked but I didn't care. We climbed into the Dodge and Doyle lit up one more cigarette before starting the engine. Windows down, night air rushing in, we pulled out of the lot and headed back toward Greenway and Tatum. "That was..." I didn't have the words.

"Yeah." He knew what I meant.

We drove in comfortable silence for a while. The radio was playing low, some song about a highway and a woman waiting at the end of it. Doyle had his arm out the window, smoke trailing back into the night. "Thanks, Doyle. For tonight."

He glanced over, grinned. "Don't thank me. Just don't embarrass me next time."

Next time. I liked the sound of that. Already I wanted to go back. I was thinking about Michelle and her number on that napkin. I was planning what I'd wear, what I'd say, how I'd act. Doyle had opened a door to a world I didn't know existed and I wanted to walk through it again.

"Rockin Rodeo was just the start," he said, like he was reading my mind. "There's Lucky's over near Grand Ave. They've got an arena out back where guys ride bulls on amateur night. And Harold's up in Cave Creek, more of a rodeo crowd. Cowboys who actually work ranches, not just guys who dress the part. That's our circuit now. Every weekend, sometimes during the week if the shift ends right."

Our circuit. I liked the sound of that too. The idea that there was a world out there, a whole network of bars with people and possibilities, and Doyle was going to show me all of it. He knew everyone. He belonged everywhere. And now, maybe, I could belong too. "You think Michelle will actually pick up when I call?" I asked.

He grinned in the darkness, cigarette glowing between his fingers. "Only one way to find out, Hanson."

I woke up the next morning with my head pounding and my mouth tasting like an ashtray. My clothes from last night were piled on the floor and I could smell the smoke from across the room. That was just how it was back then. You went to a bar, you came home reeking. Your clothes, your hair, everything. You'd wake up the next day smelling like you'd slept in a chimney. But I was smiling.

Doyle was already up, banging around in the kitchen. Making coffee in his chaotic way, spilling grounds on the counter, leaving the milk out. I shuffled in and sat down at the table without saying anything.

He poured two cups, pushed one across to me, and sat down across the table. We drank in silence. We didn't need to talk about it. We both knew what had happened, what had changed. I wasn't just his coworker anymore. I wasn't just his roommate.

I was his friend learning to be something more than what he'd been. "Same time next week?" I asked.

"Same time next week."

I did call Michelle. That Tuesday, after work, hands shaking a little as I dialed. She picked up on the third ring and sounded genuinely happy to hear from me. We made plans for that weekend. Dinner first, then back to Rockin Rodeo so I could show her what I'd learned. It didn't work out between us in the end. She moved to Tucson a few months later for a job, and long distance wasn't something either of us wanted to try. But she was the first. The first girl I met in Doyle's world, the first number I got at a country bar, the first proof that maybe I could do this after all.

That was the first night. There'd be a hundred more just like it. Rockin Rodeo, Lucky's, Harold's. The smoke, the music and the girls in their Rockies. Longnecks and Jim Beam. Doyle working the room while I learned to do the same. Sometimes I'd succeed, sometimes I'd fail, but I was always learning. I was always watching him trying to figure out how he made it look so easy.

The good times rolled out in front of us like a highway with no end.

At least that's what I thought. You never know when you're living the best years of your life. You just live them and assume there's more to come. You wake up hungover and smelling like smoke and you think this is just the beginning. You think there's a thousand more Friday nights waiting for you driving in that messy Dodge. A thousand more conversations at the bar while Doyle reads the room like scripture. That's what makes it hurt so much later. The not knowing. The thinking it would last forever.

But I'm getting ahead of myself. That morning, sitting in the kitchen with bad coffee and a hangover, all I knew was that I wanted more. More nights like that. More of that feeling when Michelle wrote her number on that napkin and slid it across the bar like she was handing me a ticket to a life I'd never imagined. More of everything.

Chapter Four – Ladies man

Friday nights had a rhythm. Work, shower, bar. Doyle, girls, Jim Beam, home. Repeat. It started the same way every week. Five o'clock would hit and the energy in the shop would shift. You could feel it... The last jobs getting wrapped up fast as guys were cleaning their bays with one eye on the clock. The weekend was coming and everybody knew it.

Doyle would find me in the parking lot, leaning against his Dodge with a cigarette going. He never seemed to need a shower after work. Trim guys had it easy that way. Meanwhile I'd be covered in transmission fluid, smelling like a gear box, counting the minutes until I could get home and wash the day off. "Rockin Rodeo or Lucky's tonight?" he'd ask.

"You pick."

"Rockin Rodeo. They have a better crowd on Fridays."

I'd follow him back to the apartment in my Mustang, the subwoofers rattling the seats behind me. I jumped in for a quick shower while Doyle changed his shirt and checked his hair in the mirror. He could primp when he wanted to, spending ten minutes getting those curls to do something they didn't want to do. Then we'd pile into the Dodge, garbage on the floorboards, cigarette smoke filling the cab, and head out into the Arizona night.

The sun would be setting by the time we hit the road, painting the sky orange and pink over the desert. Tim McGraw was on the stereo, windows down with warm air whipping through the cab. Doyle would be tapping the steering wheel in time with the music, grinning, already thinking about the night ahead.

That was the ritual. That was the freedom. Work hard all week, play harder on the weekend. We had money in our pockets, gas in the tank, and nowhere we needed to be except wherever the night took us. It was as simple as that.

Doyle would walk into a bar and something would happen. I don't know how else to describe it. The room would shift. Women would turn toward him like flowers toward the sun, and they wouldn't even know they were doing it. He'd find a spot at the bar, order his whiskey, light his cigarette, and within ten minutes someone would be talking to him. Someone beautiful. Someone who'd walked past me without a second glance.

I tried to figure out what he had. I watched him for months, trying to crack the code. It wasn't his looks. It wasn't money. We made roughly the same paycheck. It wasn't charm in any way I could identify or replicate. He didn't have pickup lines. He didn't have moves. He just... was.

"How do you do it?" I asked him once.

"Do what?"

"This... All of this. You walk in and they just... I don't get it."

He lit a cigarette, shrugged. "Don't know what you're talking about, Hanson."

He wasn't being humble. He genuinely didn't see it. That was part of the magic. He didn't try because he didn't think there was anything to try at. He just existed, and people wanted to be near him. I never figured it out. It is still a mystery to this day for me...

There was this routine we had. The Two Roberts. It sounds stupid, and it was. But it worked every time. We'd walk into Rockin Rodeo on a Friday night, the place packed, smoke thick enough to taste, Kenny Chesney on the overhead sound system. Girls everywhere in their Rockies and boots, hair done up, looking like they'd stepped out of a country music video. The kind of women who made me nervous just looking at them.

Doyle would spot a group. Three of them, maybe four. Standing near the dance floor, drinks in hand, scanning the room. He'd study them for a minute, reading something I couldn't see. Then he'd nod. "Watch and learn, Hanson."

He'd walk over, easy as anything. No hesitation, no rehearsed opener. Just walked up like he already knew them, like they were old friends meeting for a drink. "Hey. I'm Robert."

That grin. Those brown eyes that shouldn't have been anything special but somehow were. The girls would smile back before they even knew why. The prettiest one in the group, a blonde with freckles across her nose and legs that went on forever, was already leaning toward him. "And this is my buddy here." He'd wave me over, and I'd join the group, trying not to look as awkward as I felt. "His name's Robert too."

"No, it's not."

"You're lying."

"Shut up, that's not real."

They'd be laughing now, calling us liars, convinced we were running some kind of scam. And Doyle would just grin wider. "I'm serious. Pull out your ID, Hanson."

We'd both reach for our wallets. Hand over our driver's licenses. The girls would huddle together, comparing the names, looking back at us, looking at the IDs again. "Oh my God. It's real. You're both Robert."

"Told you."

By then we were in. That was the trick. While they were distracted by the gimmick, while they were laughing at the coincidence and checking our licenses, we'd already picked out who we wanted to talk to. Who we'd ask to dance. The game was over before they realized it had started.

"It was a stupid gimmick," I told him once, driving home.

"Yeah," he agreed. "But it worked."

It did... Every time. That night with the blonde and her friends, Doyle ended up two-stepping with her while I talked to a brunette named Casey who worked at a salon in Scottsdale. She had a sweet smile and she laughed at my jokes even when they weren't funny. We danced a few songs, traded numbers, and she called me the next week. We went out twice before it fizzled, but that was more than I would have gotten on my own.

The Two Roberts. The dumbest pickup routine in the history of bars. And it never failed. I got introduced to more beautiful women standing next to Doyle than I ever met on my own.

Of course, being introduced was different from closing the deal. Doyle would peel off with his pick of the group. I'd be left with whoever remained. Sometimes that worked out. Sometimes it didn't. The difference between us was never clearer than in those moments.

I'd approach a girl on my own and I could feel myself thinking too hard. What do I say? What do I do with my hands? Is she interested? Am I being too aggressive? Not aggressive enough? My mind would race through possibilities and outcomes and strategies, and all of that thinking would show on my face.

I remember one night at Lucky's. A pretty girl was at the bar, dark hair, nice smile. Doyle was off somewhere, so I was on my own. I walked up, opened my mouth, and what came out was, "Hi, I'm... do you want a drink? I mean, I'm Hanson. Robert. Do you come here a lot?"

She looked at me like I'd asked her to solve a math problem. "Are you okay?"

"Yeah. Fine. I just..." I was already backing away. "Never mind."

Women can smell desperation. They can smell uncertainty and they run from it. Doyle never thought about it. He just did it. He'd walk up to a woman like he was walking up to an old friend, like there was no possibility in the world that she wouldn't want to talk to him. And because he believed it, she believed it too. "You're thinking too much," he told me once, watching me crash and burn with a blonde by the pool tables.

"What am I supposed to think about?"

"Nothing. That's the point. You walk over, you say hi, you see what happens. You're not defusing a bomb, Hanson. You're talking to a girl."

Easy for him to say. He'd never defused a bomb either, but I was pretty sure he'd be good at that too. I got better over time. I learned to relax a little, to stop treating every conversation like a job interview. Some nights I'd go home with a number in my pocket. Some nights I'd even go home with company. But I was never going to be Doyle. I was a decent student, but I was never going to be the master.

The difference was simple. I approached with hope and Doyle approached with certainty. Girls can tell the difference.

The parade of women through our apartment was constant. I'd wake up on a Saturday morning, head pounding, mouth tasting like an ashtray, and stumble out to the kitchen to make coffee. Halfway through measuring the grounds, I'd hear Doyle's bedroom door open. Then footsteps in the hallway. Then a voice I didn't recognize.

"Oh. Hi. Um. I'm just going to... bathroom?"

"Down the hall. Left side."

"Thanks."

Some beautiful stranger would shuffle past me, wrapped in one of Doyle's shirts, trying not to make eye contact. I'd go back to making coffee like this was normal. For our apartment, it was.

Doyle would emerge eventually, usually around noon. He'd find me on the couch, watching TV, nursing my hangover. The girl would be gone by then, or sometimes still there, sitting at the kitchen table drinking the coffee I'd made, waiting for him to wake up.

He treated them all well. That was the thing. Some guys, the ones who could get women like Doyle could, they treated them poorly. Like they were conquests, trophies or notches on a bedpost. Doyle was never like that. He was charming at eight in the morning when his hair was a mess and he hadn't brushed his teeth yet. He'd make them laugh, ask about their night, offer to make breakfast even though his cooking was terrible. He made them feel like they mattered, even the one-night stands. "Doesn't it bother you?" I asked him once. "The way they just... come and go?"

"Why would it bother me?"

"I don't know. Doesn't it feel empty?"

He thought about it. "Nope. It feels like living."

Maybe he was right. Maybe I was the one doing it wrong, looking for meaning in everything when sometimes things just were what they were. A night with a connection creating a memory. Then everyone moves on.

One Saturday I woke up to another model in her underwear stepping out of my bathroom. She stopped dead when she saw me in the hallway.

"Oh God. Sorry. Robert said I could use..."

"It's fine."

"Your bathroom's really clean."

"I know." I was too tired to explain the pig versus clean freak dynamic. "Coffee?"

She nodded, wrapped a towel around herself and sat at the kitchen table. Doyle came out a few minutes later and did his usual thing. He kissed her on the forehead, poured himself a cup like any other morning.

He'd volunteer my bathroom to the girls without asking. He would just tell them to use the clean one down the hall. He never asked permission. It never occurred to him that he should. In Doyle's world, what was his was everyone's, and what was mine was his to offer to women anyways... dudes were not allowed to use my bathroom.

Another morning, I was in the shower when I heard my bathroom door open. A woman's voice said, "Oh, sorry, I thought this was empty." The shadow behind the curtain hesitated. "Should I wait?"

"Just... give me a minute."

I finished the fastest shower of my life, wrapped a towel around myself, opened the curtain to find a blonde I'd never seen before waiting patiently by the sink. "I'm the roommate," I said.

"I figured." She smiled. "Doyle said you'd be cool with it."

I was cool with it. It was a running joke now that I didn't mind. At work Doyle would tell me again how my toilet seat was getting more ass than me. I would smile and laugh it off... seeing a train of beautiful women in their underwear was something I didn’t have a hard time accepting.

There was a girl named Rita. She was around for a while. Long enough that I started to think she might be different. Long enough that Doyle started acting differently. I don't remember exactly where he met her. One of the bars, probably. Rockin Rodeo or Lucky's. She was pretty in a real way, not done up like the country girls usually were. She had brown hair, smart eyes with a laugh that sounded like she meant it. She pushed back on Doyle's bullshit, which most girls didn't. She called him out when he was being an ass, which he sometimes was.... and he seemed to like it.

They dated for maybe two months. In Doyle time, that was an eternity. I got used to seeing her around the apartment, her things appearing on the kitchen counter, her voice in the mornings. She'd make breakfast on Sundays. Actual breakfast, not the cereal and coffee that passed for food in our kitchen. Eggs, bacon and toast. The whole apartment would smell like dinner.

She had this way of handling Doyle. When he'd get too loud, too full of himself, she'd just look at him. One eyebrow raised, arms crossed. And he'd actually dial it back. I'd never seen anyone do that before. I'd never seen Doyle dial anything back for anyone. I started to think maybe this was it. Maybe Doyle had found the one who would slow him down. And then out of nowhere it ended.

I never got the full story. Doyle wasn't the type to dissect his relationships. One day she was around, the next she wasn't. "What happened with Rita?" I asked.

He shrugged, lit a cigarette. "Didn't work out."

"She seemed good for you."

"Yeah." He exhaled smoke toward the ceiling. "Maybe that was the problem."

I didn't push. You learned when not to push with Doyle. But I wondered if he'd gotten bored, scared or just couldn't help himself when other women crossed his path. Maybe it was all three.

We tried a new bar after that. We ended up at this dump of an Irish bar that was closer to the apartment. It had an annoying live band where the singer would insist you chug your drink if he caught you looking at him. It was a huge spectacle that I didn't care for. Either way, it was a shorter drive home, which Doyle said was the reason, but I knew it was to avoid running into Rita. The country bars were her territory now. That's how it works after a breakup. Somebody gets the bars at least for a period of unknown time.

The Irish place was different from what we were used to. It had dark wood instead of neon. Celtic knots on the walls instead of wagon wheels. A quieter crowd that was older and more serious about their drinking. Doyle discovered Guinness there and he damn near drowned in it. He'd sit at the bar working through pints, that dark beer leaving a foam mustache on his lip that he'd wipe away with the back of his hand. Three pints, four pints, five. The bartender knew his name by the end of the first week.

The new bar came with a new crowd and new girls. The women at the Irish place were different too. They were less done up, less country. More likely to want a real conversation than a two-step. Doyle adapted, like he always did. It was a different style with the same results.

I thought maybe Rita would be the one to change him, but Doyle wasn't ready to stop. He was still looking for something. He just didn't know what yet.

Doyle wasn't all charm. He had an edge. Three or four Jim Beams into the night, that edge would come out. He'd stir the pot just to watch it bubble. At times he could start friendly trouble for no reason except that he couldn't help himself.

It was obnoxious and juvenile. It could have gotten him punched more than once. But that was Doyle. He couldn't resist poking the bear. He'd walk right up to the line of acceptable behavior and then take one more step just to see what would happen.

One night at Harold's, this guy got in his face. He was a big guy with a cowboy hat that looked like he wrestled steers for fun. His girlfriend had been talking to Doyle for maybe five minutes, nothing serious, just conversation. But the boyfriend didn't see it that way. "What the hell do you think you're doing?"

Doyle stayed calm. Always calm. "Just talking, man."

"That's my girl."

"Didn't know she was yours. She didn't mention it."

"She's wearing my ring."

Doyle looked at her hand without a ring. Then looked back at the guy. "You might want to have a conversation about that."

The guy's face went red. For a second I thought he was going to swing. I was already calculating angles, figuring out how to pull Doyle out of there before things got ugly. But the girlfriend grabbed her boyfriend's arm and dragged him away, hissing something in his ear. The guy shot Doyle one last look and let himself be pulled toward the door. Doyle was already ordering another round. "That could have gone bad," I said.

"Eh... could have." He took a sip of his beer. "But it didn't."

He could read people. That was part of it. He knew when to push and when to back off. He knew which guys were all bark and which ones would actually throw a punch. And he knew how to defuse a situation with a joke or make it worse with a word, depending on what he felt like doing.

There was only one time I thought we were actually in trouble. Some ranch hand at Harold's, big as a house, didn't appreciate Doyle's sense of humor. I don't even remember what Doyle said. Something about the guy's belt buckle, probably. The ranch hand grabbed Doyle by the shirt, lifted him half off his barstool. I was already on my feet, calculating how bad this was going to hurt to be in a full-scale bar fight.

Doyle didn't flinch. He looked the guy dead in the eyes and said, "Brother, if you're gonna hit me, hit me. But you're gonna have to buy me a drink after."

The guy stared at him for a long moment. Then he started laughing. Put Doyle down, slapped him on the back hard enough to rattle his teeth, and bought us both a round. They were trading stories like old friends by the end of the night. He could talk his way into anything and out of everything. That was his gift. That was his curse too. But I didn't know that part yet.

I learned a lot from watching Doyle. Not everything he taught me was intentional. He taught me that looks aren't everything. That confidence is its own language. And that people respond to how you feel about yourself more than how you actually look or what you say. He taught me to relax and to stop treating every interaction like a test I might fail. To ask questions and actually listen to the answers. To be present instead of calculating.

He taught me that you can walk into a room like you own it even if you've never been there before. That certainty is contagious. That a smile at the right moment is worth more than a hundred clever lines. "Stop leading with compliments," he told me once. "Girls hear that crap all day. Ask her something real. What does she do? What does she love? What makes her laugh? People want to be seen, Hanson. Not admired. Seen..."

I filed that away... I used it and it helped. What I could never learn was the effortlessness. The thing that made it look so easy. I could copy his techniques, mimic his approach and use his lines. But I couldn't replicate the essence. I was always trying while he never had to try.

Still, there was value in being in his orbit. Girls would talk to me because I was with Doyle. Some of them stayed because I was different. Steadier and that I was more interested in actually getting to know them. I got the overflow, and that was enough. I wasn't going to complain about catching the passes that Doyle didn't want. He taught me how to live. I just couldn't live the way he did.

Those were the times. Friday nights at Rockin Rodeo, the floor vibrating with the bass, bodies moving under colored lights. Saturday nights at Lucky's, watching guys try to ride bulls while Doyle shouted encouragement and criticism in equal measure. Sunday nights at the Irish place, slower, quieter, Doyle working through Guinness while we talked about nothing important.

The smoke, the music and the girls in their Rockies. Longnecks and Jim Beam with American muscle juice. Doyle entertaining everyone while I watched and learned. And sometimes I got lucky in my own right. Driving home at two in the morning with the windows down and country music on the radio. Waking up at noon with a headache and a smile.

We didn't know they were numbered. Shit, at twenty-five you can miss a lot. The good times felt like they would last forever. The only thing that mattered was... money in your pocket and a best friend who could charm the world. Add in a city full of bars and women... well you can only imagine the endless possibilities. The future is something that happens to other people. You're just living it.

We were wrong about that last part. Something was coming. Something that would touch us in ways we couldn't have imagined. But not yet. For now, it was just the Two Roberts. The bars, the girls and the good times rolling out in front of us like a highway with no end. Doyle shot me that look at the end of the night, cigarette in his hand, grinning that grin. "Hell of a night, Hanson."

"Hell of a night."

"Same time next week?"

"Where else would I be?"

Chapter Five – Living the Dream

We had a rhythm that Monday through Friday we'd be at the dealership by seven, punching the clock, heading to our bays. I'd spend the day underneath cars, covered in transmission fluid and brake dust, fighting with stubborn bolts and cursing at rusted parts. Doyle would be twenty feet away in the trim section, working on door panels and dashboards with the precision of a surgeon.

After work we'd head back to the apartment. I'd shower off the day while Doyle lit a cigarette and cracked a beer. He never needed to clean up. Trim guys had it easy that way. Some nights we'd go out. Some nights we'd stay in, watching TV that Doyle ignored while he partied with whoever stopped by. The beer can towers would grow. The ashtrays would fill while the hours would disappear.

Weekends were for the bars. Rockin Rodeo on Friday, Lucky's or Harold's on Saturday. Sometimes the Irish place if we were feeling lazy. Sunday was recovery. I'd do laundry while Doyle slept until noon, then we'd start the whole thing over again.

It sounds simple because it was. Two guys in their mid-twenties with money in our pockets, no responsibilities, and nowhere we needed to be except wherever the night took us. That was the beauty of it. We didn't know how rare that was.

The Ford dealership on Bell Road was its own world. You spend more time with those guys than your family. Nine hours a day, five days a week, year after year. You learn their rhythms, their moods, their bullshit. You learn who to trust and who to watch. You learn the hierarchy without anyone explaining it.

The techs were divided by specialty. Heavy line guys like me handled the big stuff. Transmissions, engines, the jobs that left you covered in fluid and aching by the end of the day. Tune guys like Richard did the brain work. Diagnostics, electrical, the problems that required thinking more than muscle. Trim guys like Doyle handled the finesse work. Door panels, dashboards, the interior pieces that customers actually saw and touched.

You couldn't be soft in a shop. The guys would test you from day one. One guy, a young kid fresh out of tech school, made the mistake of complaining to management about the pranks. Word got around in about five minutes. After that, his life was hell. His tools would go missing. His jobs would get reassigned. Guys would "accidentally" bump into his lift when he was underneath a car. He lasted two months before he quit. Nobody felt bad about it. That's just how it worked.

Doyle figured out the game fast. In the first week, someone put a fake spider in his toolbox. Most guys would have jumped, maybe cussed, given the pranksters what they wanted. Doyle just picked up the spider, walked over to the guy who'd planted it, and dropped it in his coffee cup without saying a word. Everyone laughed. The guy never messed with Doyle again.

Stupid stuff, but it added up. If you complained, if you let it get to you, they'd do it more. That's how shops work. The only way out was through. You had to give it back twice as hard. You had to prove you could take it and dish it out. A shop will test you. If you can't take the heat, they turn it up until you can or until you quit.

Pops, as I called him had gray hair, a bad back, but hands like leather gloves from forty years of turning wrenches. He could out-flag me on his worst day. The man was a machine. I'd be struggling to hit my hours and he'd be done by three, sitting in his bay reading the paper, waiting for the next job to drop.

We had words more than once. I'd accuse him of cherry-picking the gravy jobs. He'd tell me to work faster. I started calling him Pops just to get under his skin. One time I got him good. He had this habit of keeping a deck of playing cards in his toolbox. He'd play solitaire during his lunch break, every single day. I snuck into his bay early one morning and took the queen of hearts out of the deck. Just one card. I watched him play solitaire for three days straight, getting more and more frustrated that he couldn't finish a game. When he finally figured out what happened, the look on his face was worth every bit of the ass-chewing he gave me. "You little shit," he said, but he was almost smiling.

That was when I knew I was in. You don't prank someone unless you respect them. And you don't take a prank well unless you can give it back. Pops and I understood each other after that. We still gave each other hell every day, but it was different. We were on the same team.

Doyle had proved himself to most of the techs including Richard but he still gave us both shit. "You two ever gonna grow up?" Richard would say when me and Doyle were cutting up in the parking lot.

"Not if we can help it," Doyle would answer.

Then one night Doyle invited him to a strip club... That's all it took. Richard came back a different man. He was laughing at our jokes instead of rolling his eyes. His wife, though. She never let him forget that night. She brought it up at every shop Christmas party for years afterwards.

I think about Doyle's hands more than anything else now. What they could do. You had to be skilled, doing what we did. But Doyle was an artist. There's a difference between competence and grace, and Doyle had grace.

He'd pick up a trim piece like it was made of glass. His fingers would find the clips, the fasteners, the hidden screws that held everything together. He never forced anything. He never scratched a panel or broke a tab. The pieces came apart in his hands like they wanted to, like they were cooperating with him instead of fighting.

I remember this one job. A Lincoln Town Car, top of the line. It belonged to some lawyer who was particular about everything. The door panel had a rattle that three other techs had tried to fix. They'd pulled the panel, checked the clips and put it back together. The rattle stayed and the lawyer was furious. He kept bringing it back, demanding someone fix it. Doyle took the job when nobody else wanted it. I watched him work for maybe twenty minutes. He pulled the panel slow, methodical, feeling along the edges with his fingertips. Then he stopped, reached into the door cavity and pulled out a pen. A ballpoint pen that had somehow fallen into the door, probably years ago. It had been rattling around ever since. "Found your problem," he said, holding up the pen.

The other techs couldn't believe it. They'd all pulled that panel. None of them had thought to reach deeper, to feel around in the cavity itself. Doyle just knew. His hands knew. Those hands steady as stone. Calluses from the work but not rough. There was a gentleness to them that didn't match the rest of him. When he smoked, the cigarette looked natural there, like an extension of his fingers. When he worked, the tools disappeared into his grip and became part of him. "You ever think about doing something else?" I asked him once, watching him reassemble a dashboard. "With your hands, you could do anything."

"Like what?"

"I don't know. Build furniture. Woodworking or something."

He looked at his hands like he'd never really seen them before. Turned them over, studied the calluses, the grease permanently embedded in the creases of his knuckles. "Nah," he said finally. "I like cars. I like this."

He went back to work and I went back to watching him moving with a certainty I'd never have. Making something complicated look simple. Making something broken look new.

There was another job I remember. An electrical problem that had stumped Richard for two days. Some phantom drain that was killing the battery overnight. Richard had been through every system, checked every relay, tested every circuit. Nothing. The car just kept dying.

Doyle asked if he could take a look. Richard was frustrated enough to let him try. I watched Doyle sit in the driver's seat for maybe ten minutes, just looking at the dash, not touching anything. Then he got out, popped the hood, and started tracing wires with his fingers. Ten minutes later he found it. A pinched wire behind the wiper motor assembly that someone had replaced years ago. The insulation had worn through and was grounding out intermittently. Richard just stared at him. "How the hell did you know to look there?"

Doyle shrugged. "The wires use the same junction block. I trace them back from the junctions and then I dig deeper."

It wasn't that simple. I'd seen him do it enough times to know. He had a gift. His hands could feel things the rest of us couldn't. His brain could see connections we missed.

The dealership had characters. Every shop does, but ours had more than most. Dave ran the parts counter like it was the Roman Senate. The guy was obsessed with gladiator movies. Spartacus, Gladiator, Ben-Hur, anything with swords and sandals. He had quotes memorized. He had opinions about historical accuracy. He had theories about what Rome could teach modern America.

He'd decorated his little parts booth with Roman stuff. A miniature gladiator helmet on his desk. A poster of Russell Crowe from Gladiator on the wall. A coffee mug shaped like a Roman soldier's head. The other parts guys thought he was nuts. Dave didn't care. He knew what he liked. "You know what Marcus Aurelius said about adversity?" Dave would start, and the whole shop would groan.

Doyle loved giving him shit about it. They'd go back and forth for hours, Dave defending the honor of ancient Rome while Doyle poked holes in everything. "Dave, you're Spartacus reborn in the wrong century," Doyle told him once.

Dave didn't miss a beat. "At least I'd have died with honor."

"I'd rather die with a beer."

That was them. That was all of us. The bullshit, the banter, the endless back and forth that made the days go faster. Richard started joining our conversations instead of hovering at the edges. He was older than us by fifteen years, married with kids, living a completely different life. But in the shop, for those nine hours, he was just another guy trying to beat flat rate and get through the day.

His wife came to pick him up once. Doyle happened to be walking through the lobby at the same time. She looked at him, looked at Richard, and said, "This is him? This is the one who corrupted you?"

Doyle put on his most innocent face. "Ma'am, I don't know what you're talking about."

Richard turned red. His wife didn't buy it for a second. But she smiled a little when she said it. Even she couldn't resist Doyle's charm completely. The service writers loved him. The customers loved him. The other techs either loved him or hated him, and the ones who hated him usually came around eventually. That was his gift. He made friends out of enemies. He made everyone feel like they were in on the joke, even when they were the joke.

Even Pops warmed up to him. The old man who gave everyone hell. He'd been there longer than most of us had been alive and he didn't suffer fools. He'd stop by Doyle's bay sometimes just to watch him work. He never said much, he just watched. Coming from Pops, that was the highest compliment you could get. "That kid's got something," Pops told me once. "Can't explain it. Either you have it or you don't. He's got it."

Coming from a man who'd seen a thousand mechanics come and go, that meant something. A dealership is its own world. The politics, the competition, the alliances and rivalries that form over years of working side by side. But through all of it, Doyle moved like water. Finding the path of least resistance. Making everything look easy.

After work, the apartment was our decompression chamber. I'd come home covered in the days work. Doyle would already be there, showered and changed or just lounging in the same clothes he'd worn to work because trim guys don't get dirty. He'd have a beer open and a cigarette going, maybe some music playing on that stereo he loved. "Hell of a day," he'd say.

"Hell of a day," I'd agree.

That was usually enough. We didn't need to dissect every job, every problem, every interaction with management. We'd left all that at the shop. Home was for something else.

People stopped by constantly. Other guys from the dealership. Friends of friends. Women Doyle had met somewhere. The apartment was never empty for long. There was always someone on that questionable couch, always a conversation happening and always something going on. The beer can towers grew throughout the week. Doyle would stack the empties in elaborate structures on the coffee table, seeing how high he could go before the whole thing collapsed. When it finally fell, usually around Thursday or Friday, he'd just start over. Building something out of nothing, even with trash. We were home one of those nights talking about nothing. "What do you think you'll be doing in ten years?" I asked him once.

"Probably this," he said. "Why change something that works?"

"Don't you want more?"

"More what?" He looked at me, genuinely curious. "I got a job I don't hate. An apartment, friends, girls and beer. What else is there?"

I didn't have an answer. Maybe there wasn't one. Maybe he was right. Maybe the thing we're all searching for is what he'd already found.

There was a night that year that captured everything. We took the Dodge to Harold's, the one out in Cave Creek where the real cowboys drank. The sun was setting over the desert, painting everything into a beautiful sunset, and Doyle was tapping the steering wheel in time with the music. Harold's was different from Rockin Rodeo or Lucky's. Less flash, more substance. The guys' boots there had real mud on them. Their hats had real sweat stains. They didn't dress like cowboys for the weekend. They were the real thing.

Doyle fit right in. That was another thing about him. He could be anywhere, with anyone, and make it look like he belonged. He'd talk horses with the ranchers, talk cars with the mechanics, talk business with the suits. Whatever world he walked into, he found a way to speak the language.

I watched him work the room that night. The same routine, the same magic. Within an hour he knew everybody's name. Within two hours he was buying drinks for strangers who felt like old friends. Within three hours he had a girl on each arm and a crowd around him, laughing at something he'd said.

He told a story about a customer at the dealership. Some rich guy who'd brought in his Navigator because the seat warmer wasn't working. Doyle had fixed it in five minutes. The guy had tipped him a hundred dollars. The way Doyle told it, with gestures and the voices along with perfect timing, you'd think it was the funniest thing that had ever happened. It was all about the way he told it, he was such a story teller and the environment was prime for it.

The smoke was thick enough to taste. The long necks were cold. The jukebox played nothing but country. I recall, George Strait singing 'Amarillo by morning' afterwards. I stood at the edge of his orbit, content to be there, watching the show. "You ever get tired of it?" some girl asked me. "Being his sidekick?"

I thought about it. I guess I never considered myself a side kick. Rather just part of the entourage...

"No."

"Why not?"

"Because it's a never-ending show... it's like this 24/7."

She didn't understand. Most people didn't. They saw me in Doyle's shadow and assumed I was jealous, pathetic, or settling for less than I deserved. They didn't get it. I wasn't completely in his shadow. I had my own thing too but shadows were ok when the light was that good. Doyle taught me things without ever trying to teach me. Before I met him, I was careful and guarded. The kind of guy who calculated every move, weighed every risk and played it safe. I'd approach a girl like I was walking through a minefield. I'd order the same beer every time because I knew I liked it. I'd take the same route to work, eat at the same restaurants... live in the same comfortable rut. Doyle didn't have a rut. He had a life. Watching him was like watching someone play a game you didn't know existed or how it ended. He took chances, talked to strangers and said yes to things that scared him... and no to things that bored him. He lived like someone who understood that time was finite, even though he never said it that way. "What's the secret, Doyle? How do you do it?"

"Do what?"

"All of it. Live like this."

He blew smoke toward the ceiling, he thought about it for a second. "You just do it, Hanson. You stop thinking and you just do it."

It was easy for him to say. His brain wasn't wired for overthinking. Mine sure was but man I tried. I watched him and I tried to absorb whatever I could. Some of it stuck.

I started talking to people I would have ignored before. I started saying yes to things that scared me. I was living a little, a little braver. I was never going to be Doyle. My brain wouldn't allow it. But I could be a better version of myself. He didn't lecture or give advice unless you asked for it. The lessons came through osmosis. Through a thousand nights of watching him work a room, charm a woman, defuse a situation, make something out of nothing. Stuff I'm still trying to learn.

Those were great memories of my life. You think the good times will go on forever because that's all you've ever known. The idea that something could come along and shatter everything doesn't happen. You don't think that one night could divide your life into before and after... you don't think about that when you're twenty-five and invincible. The days blurred together in the best way possible. Monday felt like Friday. Friday felt like it would never end. The weekends stretched out like highways with no destination, and we drove them as fast as we could. The feeling of being young, alive and certain that nothing could touch us.

One night at Lucky's, we were watching the bull riders out back in the arena. Guys getting thrown, guys getting trampled, guys walking away with broken ribs and stupid grins on their faces. I mentioned that I'd always wanted to try it. Doyle laughed. "You? On a bull?"

"What's wrong with that?"

"Nothing." He took a drag of his cigarette. "You're just too big and beautiful for it, Hanson. The bulls wouldn't know what to do with you."

"You ever ride?"

"Hell no." He shook his head. "Horses, yeah. I did some bronco riding when I was younger. But bulls? I'm not that stupid. That's for other people."

I should have left it there. But something about the way he said it made me want to prove him wrong. It made me want to try something that scared me, the way he'd lived his life. That decision would lead somewhere but that's a story for another time. You never do know when you're living the good times. You just live them, and hope they last, and one day you look back and realize they are gone.

Chapter Six - Bull Riding

The idea started at Lucky's, which should have been my first warning. Lucky's was different from the other bars on our circuit. Rockin Rodeo had the two-step crowd, the girls in their tight jeans and cowboy boots. Harold's had the ranch hands, the real cowboys who actually worked cattle for a living. But Lucky's had the arena out back. Amateur night every Saturday. Bulls and guys crazy enough to ride them.

We were inside at the bar, George Strait on the jukebox singing about looking for eight when they pull that gate. The rodeo crowd filled every booth and barstool. These weren't weekend cowboys. These were the real thing. It was a training ground for amateurs of sorts... Dusty hats, worn boots, scars they'd earned the hard way.

Doyle fit right in, of course. He always did. Leaning against the bar with a longneck in one hand and a cigarette in the other, talking to some guy about horse breeding like he'd done it his whole life. There was always more to Doyle than I knew.

I was watching the back windows, where you could see the arena lit up under the floodlights. Guys were climbing on bulls out there. Getting thrown... Getting up and climbing on again. "C'mon you ever ridden a bull?" I asked him.

Doyle turned from his conversation, followed my gaze to the arena. He shook his head. "Hell no."

"But you grew up around horses, right? Did the whole country thing?"

"Horses, yeah." He took a drag of his cigarette. "Did some bronco riding when I was younger. I broke my collarbone twice before I turned eighteen but bulls?" He shook his head again. "I'm not that stupid, Hanson. That's for other people."

"How hard can it be?"

He looked at me then. That grin started spreading across his face, the one that meant he knew something I didn't. "This is gonna be fun," he said.

Doyle tried to talk me out of it on the walk from the bar to the arena. Or maybe he was just giving me enough information to talk myself out of it. Either way, I didn't listen. "There's brave and there's stupid," he said. "I try to stay on the right side of that line."

"So which side am I on?"

"I guess we're about to find out."

The night air hit us as we stepped outside, carrying the smell of the arena with it. Dirt, manure, sweat and something else. Fear, maybe. The kind that seeps out of men who are about to do something dangerous and they know it.

Doyle walked me through his history with horses as we approached the fence. He'd grown up around them and could ride before he could drive. He did bronco riding at local rodeos when he was a teenager, back when he still thought he was invincible. Later, he learned his limits of a broken collarbone and cracked ribs, "But bulls are different," he said. "Broncos want to get you off. Bulls want to kill you after they do. That's the difference."

"You sound like you're trying to scare me."

"I'm trying to educate you." He leaned on the fence, watching a rider get thrown about four seconds in. "You're too big, Hanson. Too heavy.

Bulls don't like carrying all that weight. You need to be lighter, quicker. Built like a jockey, not a linebacker."

"So, I shouldn't try?"

"I didn't say that." He turned to me with that grin. "I said you're gonna fail. But you should still try."

He was smart enough to stay off bulls. I wasn't... That should have told me something about the difference between us. Lucky's outdoor arena was something else.

Walking through the gate felt like stepping into another world. The bar inside had been loud and smoky and full of characters, but this was the real thing. Cowboys everywhere, real ones, not the kind who dressed up for Saturday night. They moved with a specific kind of confidence, the kind that comes from doing dangerous things and surviving them.

The arena itself was bigger than I expected. It had a dirt floor, metal fencing and stands on one side for spectators. Floodlights turned night into day over the whole thing. The chutes lined up along the back, holding pens behind them where the bulls waited their turn. Everything smelled like dirt and leather along with animal sweat. George Strait had given way to Chris LeDoux over the speakers with Eight Second Ride. The anthem of everyone crazy enough to climb on one of these things.

The bulls in the holding pens were massive. I'd seen bulls before, from a distance, in fields, at state fairs. But not like this. These animals were bred for one thing, and it wasn't farming. They paced and snorted and looked at the riders with something that might have been contempt. One of them, a black monster with horns like handlebars, caught my eye through the fence. I swear he knew I was coming.

I listened to LeDoux singing about holding on, about the longest eight seconds of your life, and wondered what the hell I was doing.

Doyle knew people here too. Of course he did. He introduced me to a guy named Cal who ran the amateur nights. He explained that his buddy wanted to try his luck. Cal looked me up and down with the same expression Doyle had given me earlier. "Big boy," Cal said. "You rode before?"

"First time."

"Well." He spat tobacco into the dirt. "Everyone's gotta start somewhere. We got a spinner named Dusty who's been going easy on the new guys. Might not kill you."

"Might not" it wasn't the reassurance I was hoping for. Doyle walked me to the chutes while Cal went to get me signed up. Other riders were preparing, stretching and checking their gear. A few of them nodded at Doyle. None of them nodded at me. They knew an outsider when they saw one. "You sure about this?" Doyle asked.

I looked at the bull waiting in the chute and at the guys getting thrown in the arena. At the bullfighters dodging horns and hooves. Nothing about this seemed like a good idea. "Too late to back out now."

"It's never too late to back out. That's the smartest thing anyone ever said about bull riding."

"Did you back out? When you were bronco riding?"

He thought about it. "Twice. Once because the horse looked at me wrong. Once because I'd just watched a guy get his arm broken in three places." He lit a cigarette. "No shame in walking away, Hanson."

"You'd never let me live it down."

"That's true." He grinned. "But you'd be alive to never live it down."

The preparation was its own kind of education. Doyle walked me through the gear. The glove, rosined for grip. The rope that would wrap around my hand and the bull. The vest that might keep my ribs from caving in if I got stepped on or gored. Might... "Hold on with your legs," he said. "The rope's just for balance. Your legs are what keeps you on."

"My legs."

"Your legs." He demonstrated on the fence rail, showing me how to grip, where to put my weight. "When the bull spins, you lean into it. When he bucks, you stay centered. When he does both at the same time, which he will, you just hold on and pray."

"Great advice."

"My best advice is don't do this. But since you're doing it anyway..." He shrugged. "Tuck and roll when you fall. Get to the fence fast. The bull doesn't care that you're done. He might come after you."

We watched a few more riders while I waited for my turn. Some of them made it look easy, flowing with the animal's movement like they were dancing instead of fighting. There was a rhythm to it when it worked. The bull would spin and the rider would lean into it, staying centered, and balanced. It was man and animal moving together even though one was trying to kill the other.

Some of them got thrown in the first second, hitting the dirt before they knew what happened. One guy made it maybe five seconds before getting bucked off sideways, rolling through the dust, scrambling for the fence while the bullfighters moved in to distract the animal.

Then one guy got hooked by a horn as he was scrambling away. The horn caught him in the thigh, blood on the dirt, screaming while his friends pulled him over the fence. The bullfighters got the bull back to the chute, but the damage was done. Someone called for a medic. "Jesus," I said.

"That's why you get to the fence," Doyle said. "Fast! And that's why I don't ride bulls. There's a reason it's only eight seconds. Any longer and too many people would die."

A rider went the full eight seconds, the buzzer sounding as he leaped off and ran for safety. The crowd cheered. The guy took off his hat, waved it, grinning like he'd just won the lottery. "That's what it feels like," Doyle said. "Eight seconds of not thinking about anything except staying on. Eight seconds of being completely alive. That's why people do this."

"You miss it? The broncos?"

He was quiet for a moment. "Sometimes. But my collarbone doesn't."

My name got called. It was time to find out which side of that brave-stupid line I was on.

The chute was smaller than I expected. The bull beneath me was called Dusty, supposedly one of the gentler ones. He didn't feel gentle. He felt like thousands of pounds with barely contained rage, muscle twitching under my legs, breath coming in hot snorts. I could feel his heartbeat through my thighs, or maybe that was my own heart trying to escape through my legs. The rope was in my hand, wrapped the way Doyle had shown me. The glove was sticky with rosin. The vest felt too thin, too flimsy, a joke of protection against the horns and hooves waiting to destroy me.

Chris LeDoux was still playing over the speakers. I wasn't looking for eight. I was looking for survival. Doyle was at the fence, cigarette in hand, watching. He gave me a nod. No grin now. This was serious. "Any last advice?" I called out.

"Don't think," he said. "Just hold on."

"That's it?"

"That's everything."

One of the gate guys asked if I was ready. I nodded because I didn't trust my voice. He put his hand on the latch and yelled out, "Let's go, boys!"

The gate swung open. Everything after that was chaos. Dusty exploded out of the chute like he'd been shot from a cannon. My body snapped backward, then forward, then sideways as the bull spun. I heard the crowd yelling, the music playing, my own voice making sounds I didn't recognize. The world became a blur of dirt and sky and spinning horns. I was looking for eight, but I didn't even get four.

Three seconds in, maybe less, my grip slipped. The spin threw me sideways. I was airborne before I knew I was falling, the bull somewhere beneath me, the ground somewhere below that. Time stretched out the way it does in car accidents, long enough to think "this is going to hurt" before the impact proved me right.

I hit the dirt shoulder first, rolled like Doyle had told me, scrambled toward the fence on pure instinct. My body knew what to do even if my brain was still catching up. Get away... Get to safety! Move.

Dusty was still spinning behind me, kicking at the air where I'd been. I could hear his hooves hitting the dirt, feel the vibration through my hands as I scrambled. The bullfighter moved in, waving his arms, directing him toward the exit chute. One of them got between me and the bull, putting himself in danger so I could get clear.

I grabbed the fence and pulled myself over, falling into the dirt on the other side. I lay there for a moment, staring up at the floodlights, breathing hard, wondering if all my pieces were still attached. I was safe but covered in dirt along with being embarrassed as hell. Doyle's laugh carried across the arena, clear as a bell. I could have picked that laugh out of a stadium full of people. He was still laughing when he helped me up.

"Three seconds, Hanson. Maybe four."

"It felt longer..."

"It always does."

He brushed the dirt off my shoulder, still chuckling. I could feel the bruises already forming, the ache in my shoulder where I'd landed, the places where tomorrow's pain was already settling in. But nothing was broken or bleeding. That counted as a win. "You're too big and beautiful to be a true rider," Doyle said. "But you got balls. I'll give you that."

"Too big and beautiful?"

"Look at you." He gestured at me like I was a prize horse. "Six foot, blonde, built like a brick shithouse. Bulls don't know what to do with all that pretty. You need to be small and ugly like the rest of us."

"You're not ugly."

"I'm ugly enough to stay off bulls. That's a kind of beauty."

Some of the other riders had gathered at the fence, watching with the kind of amusement that comes from seeing someone fail the same way they once failed. One of them, an older guy with a face like a worn saddle, spit tobacco and offered his assessment. "Not bad for a first timer."

"Not bad?" I was still picking dirt out of my ears. "I lasted three seconds."

"You lasted three seconds and walked away." He shrugged. "That's better than some. I've seen guys break bones on easier bulls than Dusty."

"Everyone eats dirt their first time," another guy added. "Most don't look that pretty doing it."

There it was again. Pretty... Beautiful... Apparently my crime was being too good-looking to ride bulls. Doyle was going to milk this forever.

"He got on, though," Doyle said, throwing his arm around my shoulder. "Give him that. City boy got on a bull. More than most can say."

"More than you can say," the old cowboy pointed out.

Doyle grinned, not bothered at all. "That's because I'm smart. Hanson here's just brave."

"I thought there was a line between brave and stupid," I said.

"There is." He squeezed my shoulder. "You crossed it tonight. Welcome to the stupid side, brother."

Back inside Lucky's, the story had already started to grow. The bar felt different now. Louder, warmer, more welcoming. Maybe it was the adrenaline still pumping through my system. Maybe it was the dirt still caked in places I'd be finding for days. Maybe it was the way the cowboys looked at me now, not as an outsider but as someone who'd earned something.

We'd barely gotten our beers before Doyle was telling it to anyone who'd listen. He had that gift, the storytelling thing, where everything got bigger and better in the retelling. My three seconds became two. The fall became more spectacular. Dusty became meaner, the danger more real and the escape more miraculous. "So, I'm on the fence, and this big blonde bastard comes flying off like the bull personally offended him..."

"That's not how it happened."

"I'm telling the story, Hanson. Don't interrupt."

The bar crowd ate it up. Cowboys who'd been riding for years, who'd seen a thousand rookies fail, laughing at my expense. But it wasn't mean laughter. It was the kind that welcomed you to the club, that said you'd earned something by trying even if you'd failed spectacularly.

Someone bought me a drink. Then someone else. The longnecks kept coming, Jim Beam chasers appearing without me asking. American muscle juice, Doyle called it. The fuel of cowboys everywhere.

By the time we'd been there an hour, I'd heard a dozen stories of other first rides, other failures, other guys who'd eaten dirt and lived to laugh about it. Every one of them had their version of my night. The first ride that went wrong. The bull that threw them before they were ready. The moment they realized this sport could actually kill you. "First time I rode," one guy said, "I didn't even make it out of the chute. Bull jumped before the gate opened. Crushed my leg against the fence. It took me six months to walk right again."

"My first bull stomped on my hand after I fell off," another guy added, holding up his left hand. Two fingers bent at angles God never intended. "I still can't make a fist."

"Worth it though," the first guy said.

"Worth it," the second agreed.

They were all crazy. Every one of them. But there was something about the way they talked about it, like they'd found something worth getting hurt for. Like those eight seconds, when they happened, were worth everything that came before and after. "You know what the difference is?" one of them asked me. "Between a guy who rides once and a guy who keeps riding?"

"The guy who keeps riding is stupider?"

He laughed. "The guy who keeps riding got up and wanted to try again. Did you?"

I thought about it. The fear in the chute. The chaos of the ride. The impact of the fall. Did I want to do that again?

"Maybe," I said honestly. "Someday. But not tonight."

"Smart man." He raised his glass. "Most of us spent years before we admitted that."

Doyle clinked his bottle against mine. Alan Jackson was playing Pop a Top again. The smoke was still thick. The night was still young, even though my body felt about a hundred years old. "To the too big and beautiful," Doyle said. "May they learn their limits before the bulls teach them."

I drank to that.

We drove home in the Dodge, windows down, country music playing low. The desert night air rushed through the cab, cooling the sweat, the adrenaline and the beer. My shoulder ached where I'd hit the ground. My ribs ached where I didn't remember hitting anything. My pride ached worst of all. But something else felt different too... I felt better.

The city lights of Phoenix glowed on the horizon, getting closer with every mile. Kenny Chesney came on the radio, singing. Doyle hummed along, tapping the steering wheel with his palm. "Why'd you take me?" I asked. "You knew I'd fail."

Doyle lit a cigarette, steered with his knees for a moment while he got it going. "Because you wanted to try. That's worth something."

"Even if I sucked?"

"Especially if you sucked." He exhaled smoke into the night air.

"Anyone can do something they're good at. It takes guts to do something you know you'll fail at."

I thought about that. About all the things I'd never tried because I might not be good at them. About all the things Doyle had dragged me into. Nights in bars with conversations I never would have found on my own. He didn't just live his life. He pulled you into it and made you live too. "You're too big and beautiful," he said again, that grin in his voice. "But you tried. That's more than most people do their whole lives."

"You going to call me that forever?"

"Probably." He glanced over at me. "That bother you?"

It didn't. That was the thing. Coming from anyone else, it might have stung a bit. But from Doyle, it was something else. A nickname and a reminder as a term of endearment disguised as an insult.

"Nah," I said. "I can live with it."

"Good. Because I'm going to tell this story at your wedding someday. At your funeral and every time, we pass a rodeo sign. Every time bulls come up in conversation."

"I'm sure you will."

"Three seconds, Hanson." He held up three fingers, laughing. "Maybe four."

"Maybe four."

We drove in comfortable silence for a while. The lights of Phoenix spreading out ahead of us, the desert dark behind. The ache in my body settling into something familiar, the kind of pain that tells you you're alive. That was the night he became my brother. Not because I succeeded at something. Because I failed at something, and he was there to help me up and laugh about it. That's what brothers do. They don't just share your victories. They share your failures. They make you feel like even the worst moments are worth something because you weren't alone in them.

I learned something at Lucky's that night. I wasn't going to be Doyle. I wasn't supposed to be. I was never going to be the guy who walked into a room and owned it. I knew I wasn't gifted with his charm but that was ok. I still enjoyed being the guy at his side, the wingman... simply because it was a shit ton of fun.

But I could still try things and fail. I was able to get back up and laugh about it. That was its own kind of courage, even if it looked like stupidity from the outside. I think about that night sometimes. The smell of the arena, dirt with sweat and primal fear. The feel of the bull beneath me, all that power barely contained. The sound of Doyle's laugh carrying across the dirt when I hit the ground. I did try multiple attempts, but it didn't work out for me. To me it was the shortest bull riding career in history, but I got some good pictures doing it...

I never regretted trying either. That's the thing Doyle taught me without ever saying it directly. The trying matters. The showing up matters. The willingness to fail in front of people. To fall, get up and laugh about it. That mattered more than succeeding ever could.

Some people go their whole lives without risking anything. Without putting themselves out there or trying something that scares them. It was nice to take a risk, and it was ok if it knocked me down. I used to be one of those people who never stepped outside in fear of falling. Before all of this I may have never felt ok to fail completely and survive.

That was one of the last pure nights, before things started to change. Before Tara and before the apartment on Greenway Parkway. Before the party... the pool and the dive that changed everything.

Chapter Seven - Tara

I saw her first, but it didn't matter. It never did. We were at Rockin Rodeo on a Friday night, same as always. Smoke thick, music loud, girls in their Rockies and boots moving through the crowd. Doyle was holding his own at the bar, telling some story I'd heard a dozen times to people who hadn't. I was nursing a beer, watching the room, doing my usual wingman routine. That's when I noticed her.

Dark hair, darker eyes. Sitting at the end of the bar by herself, which was unusual. Girls that pretty didn't stay alone long at any bar... let alone Rockin Rodeo. She had a drink in front of her, something clear with a lime, and she was watching the room the way I was watching it. Taking it in. Deciding what to make of it.

I thought about going over and trying the Two Roberts routine solo, which never worked as well. I thought about a lot of things in the thirty seconds it took Doyle to notice where I was looking. "Who's she?" he asked. "Don't know yet."

"You going over there?"

I was about to say yes when he pushed off the bar and headed in the direction himself with the same confidence as always... That easy go lucky stride. It was a mysterious dumbfounded certainty that whoever he approached would be glad he did.

But he stopped before he got there. Just for a second and he adjusted his collar. He ran a hand through his hair. I'd never seen him do that before... Not for a girl. That should have been my first clue. The ones who made him hesitate were the dangerous ones.

Her name was Tara and she didn't fall for Doyle immediately. I watched from across the bar as he worked his charm. The smile, the lean, the eye contact that made women feel like they were the only person in the room. All his usual tricks. The body language that said "I'm interested but not desperate." The jokes that landed perfectly because he timed them that way. The attention that made women feel like the center of the universe.

She smiled and talked back while seeming interested enough. But she didn't move closer when he leaned in. She didn't touch his arm when she laughed or give him the signals he was used to getting, the ones that meant the deal was done and all that was left was deciding whose place to go to.

She held back and kept a barrier between them that Doyle's charm couldn't seem to penetrate. And instead of losing interest, the way he usually did when things got difficult, he tried harder. He leaned in more and worked angles I'd never seen him work before. She made him work for it and somehow, that made him want her more.

When Doyle came back to my end of the bar twenty minutes later, he didn't have a number. He didn't have a promise to meet up later. All he had was a name. "Tara," he said, like he was trying out how it sounded.

"Struck out?"

"She said maybe she'd be here next Friday." He took a long pull from his beer. "Maybe."

I almost fell off my barstool. Doyle didn't get maybes. He got a yes. He got phone numbers, addresses and women following him to the parking lot. Maybe... was a foreign language. "You, okay?"

He was quiet for a moment. Watching her across the bar, where she'd gone back to sipping her drink and surveying the room. "Yeah," he said finally. "I think I'm gonna come back next Friday."

He'd never chased anyone. He didn't have to. But Tara made him chase her. That was different and new. That was... looking back on it, the beginning of the end.

Over the next few weeks, Doyle was a different person. He kept bringing her up. Tara said this. Tara thinks that. Tara has this job, this opinion, this way of looking at things. I heard more about Tara in those weeks than I'd heard about any other woman in the time I'd known him.

And he kept going back. Every Friday, sometimes Saturday too. To Rockin Rodeo, hoping she'd be there. She usually was... And slowly, week by week, the maybes turned into a yes. The distance turned into closeness. The woman who'd made him work started letting him in. I noticed the changes in Doyle before I really understood them. He was checking his hair before we left the apartment, spending ten minutes in front of the mirror when he used to spend thirty seconds. He wasn't flirting with other girls at the bar anymore. When someone pretty walked by, his eyes stayed on Tara instead of following the movement.

Then one night, he did something I'd never seen him do. He asked me for advice. "What do you think I should do?"

"About what?"

"Tara. She's..." He struggled with the words. "I don't know. Different."

I almost dropped my beer. Doyle asking for advice about a girl. In the entire time I'd known him, he'd never needed help with women. Women were the one thing he understood completely, instinctively, without effort. And now he was sitting on our questionable couch, cigarette forgotten between his fingers, asking me what to do. "Just be yourself," I said, because that's what you say.

"I've been being myself. That's the problem. She sees through it."

"Sees through what?"

"The bullshit." He finally took a drag of his cigarette. "She knows when I'm putting on a show. She doesn't like it. She wants... I don't know what she wants."

"Maybe she just wants the real you."

He thought about that. Really thought about it. "That's what scares me."

When a guy like Doyle starts asking for advice about a girl, you know something's different. When he admits he's scared, you know the world has turned upside down. I didn't have good advice to give him. I wasn't any better at this stuff than he was. I was probably worse. But I listened, and sometimes that's what people need. Someone to hear them say the things they're afraid to say out loud. Someone to make the scary thoughts real by speaking them into existence.

A few weeks later, Doyle brought her to the apartment. I'd seen her at the bar, watched them together from a distance. But this was the first time I really met her. I really had a chance to talk to her and I understood what had him so twisted up.

She was twenty-two, dark-haired, and a knockout. That much was obvious. But there was more to her than that. She was smart, really smart, in a way that showed when she talked. She had opinions about things and wasn't afraid to argue with Doyle about them. She pushed back when he tried to charm his way out of a conversation. She called him on his bullshit in a way that made him laugh instead getting of defensive. "So you're the famous Hanson," she said that first morning, sitting at our kitchen table in one of Doyle's shirts. "Robert talks about you all the time."

"All lies... probably."

"He said you were funnier than him." She smiled. "I'm starting to think he was right."

Doyle laughed from the kitchen where he was attempting to make coffee. "Don't encourage him."

I liked her. That's the hard part to remember now. I actually liked her. She was easy to talk to, genuinely interested in what I had to say, not just waiting for Doyle to come back and entertain her. She asked about my work, my life and my own romantic disasters. She listened like it mattered.

She started staying most nights after that. Her things appeared around the apartment in stages. First a toothbrush. Then some clothes in Doyle's closet. Then a makeup bag in the bathroom. Soon she was there more often than not, practically living with us even though her name wasn't on the lease.

And then something miraculous happened. I came home from work one day and stopped dead in the hallway. Something was different. Something was wrong. The apartment smelled... clean. Not just absence of bad smell, but actual cleanliness. Like someone had used actual cleaning products.

I followed my nose to Doyle's bathroom. The door was open. The toilet was white. The sink gleamed. The floor looked like a floor instead of a science experiment. "Doyle," I called out. "Did Tara... did she clean your bathroom?"

He appeared in the doorway, looking almost embarrassed. "She said she couldn't take it anymore."

"No woman has ever loved you that much."

"Shut up, Hanson."

But he was grinning. And I knew, standing there looking at that spotless bathroom, that this was serious. No casual hookup cleans a man's bathroom. No temporary fling scrubs a toilet that had seen what Doyle's toilet had seen. Tara had crossed a line that no other woman had crossed. She'd looked at the disaster that was Robert Doyle's personal hygiene and decided to fix it instead of running away. I knew then that things were going to change. I just didn't know how much.

Over the following months, Doyle transformed. He was still the same guy underneath. Still charming, still funny and the center of attention wherever we went. But the edges were softening. The wildness was fading. He was settling into something I'd never seen from him before.

Our circuit died first. The Friday nights at Rockin Rodeo, the Saturday nights at Lucky's or Harold's. The bar hopping, the girl chasing, the Two Roberts routine. All of it faded away as Tara became the center of his world.

I hadn't realized how much those nights meant to me until they were gone. The smoke, the music and the possibility of anything happening. The way Doyle and I would walk into a place and own it, even when we didn't belong there. The stories we'd tell on the drive home, embellishing every detail, making everything sound better than it was.

That was over now. That part of our lives was closing, chapter by chapter, as Tara rewrote the story. "Are we going to Rockin Rodeo tonight?" I asked one Friday.

"Nah. Tara wants to hit the Irish place. Shorter drive home."

"Since when do you care about the drive home?"

He just shrugged. That was the answer. He cared because she cared. He wanted what she wanted. The country bars were too smoky, too loud, too full of women who might remind Tara that Doyle had a past. The Irish bar was easier and quieter while being closer to the apartment.

I missed the country music. I laughed at myself... I missed George Strait, the two-step and the girls in their Rockies. But I went to the Irish bar because that's where Doyle went now, and Doyle was my best friend. That's what you do.

The parties at the apartment slowed down too. The revolving door of visitors, the beer can towers, the girls asking to use my bathroom. All of it faded as Tara became a constant presence. She didn't like the chaos. She preferred quiet nights, the three of us watching TV and hanging out. She preferred a clean apartment and a boyfriend who came home at a reasonable hour. The apartment felt emptier without the noise. I told myself I was happy for him. Mostly I was...

Doyle took Tara to meet his parents. I heard about it afterward, sitting at the bar at the Irish place. He was working through his third Guinness, which had become his drink since Tara decided longnecks were too country for the new spots they frequented. "How'd it go?"

"Mom loved her." He was grinning, that genuine grin that didn't have any performance in it. "You should've seen her face, Hanson. She hugged Tara like she was already family. Asked her all these questions about her job and her life and where she grew up. By the end of dinner, they were making plans to go shopping together."

His mom had always worried about him. I knew that without him saying it. A mother knows her son, and Sylvia had watched her boy become a charmer, a ladies' man, a guy who never stayed anywhere long enough to build anything. She'd seen the parade of women, heard about the bar nights and the parties. She'd probably lay awake wondering if her son would ever settle down or if he'd spend his whole life chasing the next good time.

Seeing him show up with a real girlfriend, someone he was serious about, must have felt like a miracle. Like finally, after all those years of worrying, her prayers had been answered. "And Steve?"

Doyle shrugged. "Steve is Steve."

That was all he ever said about his stepfather. Steve was Steve. Cold, distant, not really interested in the kid who wasn't his. Doyle had made his peace with it years ago, or at least he pretended he had. Steve's opinion didn't matter. Sylvia's opinion did... And Sylvia loved Tara.

"She asked when I was going to bring her back," Doyle said. "Mom, I mean. Not Tara. Although Tara wants to go back too."

"Sounds like it went well."

"Yeah." He stared into his Guinness. "It did. It really did."

I watched him sitting there, this guy who never planned beyond the next weekend, actually thinking about something that mattered. Something that might last. Tara had given him that. The ability to see past tomorrow, to imagine a future worth building toward.

A few weeks later, Doyle opened up about where things were heading.

We were on the couch late one night, the apartment quiet, Tara was asleep in his room. One of those nights where neither of us could sleep and neither of us wanted to be alone with our thoughts. He had a cigarette going, the smoke curling toward the ceiling, and that faraway look in his eyes. "You ever think about getting a place with someone, Hanson?"

"I haven't found the right someone yet."

"Yeah." He took a drag, held it, exhaled. "I think maybe I have."

He wasn't talking about marriage. He wasn't there yet, and maybe never would be. Doyle wasn't the kind of guy who thought about rings, ceremonies and forever. But an apartment together, a place of their own, a step toward something real. That he could see.

"She wants to find a place," he said. "Something nicer than this. Something with a good pool. She keeps talking about pools."

"You two going to move in together?"

"Maybe." Another drag. "Probably. She practically lives here anyway. Might as well make it official."

He'd never talked about the future before. He was always about right now, this moment, this night. But Tara made him think ahead. At least a little. At least one step at a time.

"I'm happy for you," I said. And I meant it.

"Yeah?" He glanced over at me. "You'd be, okay? Me moving out?"

"Lease is up in a few months anyway. I can figure something out."

"You could come with us. Get a three bedroom."

I smiled, but we both knew that wasn't going to happen. Doyle and Tara needed their own space. Their own life. I was always going to be welcome, but I wasn't going to be part of what they were building. That was for the two of them.

"I'll be fine," I said. "You go build something good."

The nights out became three instead of two. Me, Doyle and Tara at the Irish bar, working through Guinness and whatever the special was. The place was darker than the country bars, quieter, the music was more of a more background than feature. The crowd was different too. Older, calmer, people who were past the stage of looking for someone to take home.

I watched them together and tried not to feel like a third wheel. I tried not to notice how his hand always found her knee under the bar, how she leaned into him when she laughed, how they had their own language now, inside jokes I wasn't part of. The way she'd say something and he'd crack up, and I'd ask what was funny, and they'd say "you had to be there," even though I was right there.

It wasn't their fault. That's just what happens when two people fall into each other. The rest of the world fades. Inside jokes get created and a private language develops. Anyone on the outside, no matter how close they used to be, becomes a visitor in a country where they don't speak the native tongue.

"You okay over there, Hanson?" Tara asked. "We're not ignoring you, are we?"

"I'm fine. You two do your thing. I gotta get out more myself so this can be a double date not a third wheel party."

"You're part of the thing." She reached across Doyle to squeeze my arm. "Right, Robert?"

Doyle nodded. "Always."

She meant it. At the time, I think she really meant it. She tried to include me, asked about my week, remembered details I'd mentioned months before. She never made me feel like I was in the way. She never acted like she was waiting for me to leave so she could have Doyle to herself. But it was different now. The Two Roberts were becoming Doyle and Tara, plus Hanson. I finished my beer and thought about how quiet the apartment would be when he moved out. I thought about Friday nights alone, no one to drag me to bars I wouldn't go to otherwise. I needed a new wingman...

The apartment had felt too small when we first moved in. Two guys crammed into a two-bedroom, bumping into each other. Now it was going to feel enormous. All that space with no one to fill it. It was the end of an era that I hadn't realized was ending until it was almost gone.

Looking back now, I can see things I didn't see then. The way Tara checked her phone a lot, even when we were all together. The way she talked about money sometimes, about wanting nice things, about being "stuck" in situations that didn't offer enough. The way her eyes would light up when Doyle mentioned the expensive apartment she'd found, the one with the pool area they called the beach.

I didn't see it as warning signs. I saw it as normal. Everyone wants nice things. Everyone checks their phone and people dream of something better than what they have. That's just being human. But there was something else there too. Something behind those dark eyes that I couldn't quite name. The same sharpness that had made her resist Doyle's charm at first combined with her ability to see through his bullshit. That same quality could cut other ways too.

I didn't see it then or maybe I didn't want to see it. Doyle was happy. Happier than I'd ever seen him. He was building something, planning something, becoming something more than the guy who lived for the moment. How do you look at your best friend in that state and say you don't trust his girlfriend?

You don't... You keep your mouth shut. You hope you're wrong. You tell yourself that whatever doubts you have are just whack-a-doodle. They are just the fear of change, or the normal resistance of your wingman leaving the rotation. I hoped I was wrong about her. For a long time, I thought I was.

Those months with Tara, Doyle was genuinely happy. I'd never seen him like that before. Planning, hoping, believing in something beyond tomorrow. She gave him that. Whatever else she did later, whatever darkness came after, she gave him that first. The ability to imagine a future worth having. The desire to be more than what he was.

They were looking at apartments all over the place and especially in Scottsdale. They were gravitating toward a place on Greenway Parkway. It was a luxury apartment complex with a pool area they called "the beach." There was sand around the pool area, cabanas, lounge chairs arranged like you were at a resort instead of an apartment complex in Phoenix. Doyle couldn't stop talking about it.

Every time he came home from looking at the place, he had more details. The kitchen with the granite counters. The walk-in closet Tara had already claimed. The patio that had a great view of the courtyard. But mostly, always, he talked about the pool. "You should see it, Hanson. They trucked in actual sand. There's a bar by the water. The whole thing looks like something out of a magazine."

He was like a kid describing Disneyland. This pool, this beach, this place where he and Tara would build their life together. He'd never cared about stuff like that before. He never wanted anything nice enough to get excited about losing it. But Tara had changed that too. She'd given him something to want, and the pool was part of that dream.

He was thinking ahead now. Not about marriage, he wasn't there yet. But about building something nice. It was about having a place that was his and Tara's, not just a bachelor pad he shared with a roommate. It included growing up in a way he'd never considered before.

Everything was coming together for him. That's what made what happened next so hard to accept. He was so close to having everything he wanted. The apartment, the girl, that pool he kept talking about. The pool he loved so much would be the thing that destroyed him. I just didn't know it yet. None of us did.

Chapter Eight – The Roberts Part Ways

We were at the Irish bar when he told me. Tara was there, sitting close to him in the booth, with her hand on his knee under the table. I'd gotten used to seeing them like that. Attached as a unit. "We found a place," Doyle said.

"Yeah?"

"Greenway Parkway... luxury apartments. You gotta see this pool, Hanson." He was grinning like a kid on Christmas morning. "They've got sand around it. It's like a beach. It's like living at a resort."

I hadn't seen him that excited about anything in a long time. Maybe ever. He was leaning forward, hands moving as he talked, painting a picture of this place like it was paradise. The pool, the cabanas and the lounge chairs. The way the sand felt under your feet. The shallow end that sloped down into the water like you were walking into the ocean.

"I'm sorry, buddy," he said, and his face got serious for a moment. "I would renew, but we're going places."

The lease at Greenway and Tatum was up next month anyway. We both knew this was coming. I had known it since Tara started leaving her things at the apartment, since she cleaned his bathroom and he started talking about the futures plans with next steps. This was just the official announcement of something that had been happening for months. "It's good," I said. "I'm happy for you."

And I was. There was something else too, something that settled in my chest like a weight. But I smiled and raised my glass and told him the place sounded amazing because it did. And because that's what you do when your best friend tells you he's building a life with someone.

Tara was beaming beside him. This was what she wanted. The nice apartment, the pool, the life they were going to have together. She'd pulled him toward something, and he'd gone willingly. I couldn't blame her for that. I couldn't blame either of them.

"You'll come over all the time," Doyle said. "We'll have people over. Pool parties. The whole thing."

"Yeah," I said. "Sounds good."

I knew it was coming but it hit differently when he said it out loud.

The weeks before the move had a strange quality to them. The apartment at Greenway and Tatum felt different, like it was already becoming a memory while we were still living in it. Doyle packed slowly, his things disappearing into boxes one by one. The mess got smaller. His room got emptier. The walls started showing where posters used to hang.

We didn't talk about it much. What was there to say? He was moving on. I wasn't sure what I was doing... probably staying put. That was the whole story.

One night I found him wrapping his stereo in blankets, treating it like fine China. The thing was worth maybe two hundred bucks, but he loved it more than most people loved their cars.

"You gotta take that couch or get rid of it," I told him. "I don't want anything except what's in my bedroom. God only knows what happened on that furniture when I was sleeping."

He laughed. He knew exactly what had happened on that furniture. The couch had seen things no piece of furniture should see. Women whose names we'd forgotten by morning. Parties that went until sunrise.

Beer spills and cigarette burns along with moments neither of us would ever admit to out loud. "Fair enough," he said. "That couch has earned its retirement."

"Retirement... Yeah right."

"Dumpster retirement."

"Better than it deserves."

He grinned at me across the half-packed room. For a second it felt like old times. Two Roberts, giving each other shit, the way it had always been. Then he went back to wrapping the stereo, and I went back to my room, and the moment passed like all the others were passing.

Moving day arrived hot and bright, the Arizona sun was already brutal by nine in the morning. Doyle's Dodge sat in the lot, bed open, ready to swallow whatever we threw into it. The hay was still there underneath everything, part of the truck's permanent identity. You could pile furniture on top of it, but the hay remained. That truck would smell like hay until the day it died.

Tara showed up early, hair pulled back, ready to work. She surprised me with that. I expected her to direct traffic while we did the heavy lifting, but she grabbed boxes and carried them outside alongside us. Smaller boxes, sure. The ones without much weight. But she was there, sweating in the morning heat, wanting this move to happen. Invested in getting Doyle out of this apartment and into their new life.

The apartment emptied out in stages. First Doyle's bedroom, the boxes he'd packed over the last few weeks. Then the kitchen stuff he was keeping, the plates and cups that weren't too chipped to use. Then the living room, piece by piece, until there was nothing left but echoes and carpet stains.

The couch went last. Doyle and I wrestled it outside, scraping walls, nearly dropping it twice. The thing was heavier than it looked, or maybe we were just tired. By the time we got it to the dumpster, we were both sweating through our shirts.

He didn't just toss it in. He stopped for a moment, looking at it. This ugly, questionable, history-laden piece of furniture that had been the center of our lives for a time. Beer can towers had been built on that couch. Stories had been told. Women had been charmed. It was disgusting, perfect and irreplaceable. Doyle gave it a salute.

"Fuck it," he said.

Then he heaved it over the edge. It landed with a thud that sounded final. It signaled an end of an era. We stood there for a second, looking at it sitting vertically in the dumpster. Then he slapped my shoulder and headed back toward the apartment. "We're gonna lose that deposit," I said, following him.

"No question."

"Your room looks like a crime scene."

"It's not that bad."

"There are stains, Doyle. Stains I don't want to know about."

He just grinned. We both knew the cleaning deposit was gone the moment he moved in. That bathroom alone had probably violated several health codes before Tara got to it.

"Good luck getting your deposit back at the new place," I said.

"Different man now, Hanson. Tara's got me trained."

"We'll see how long that lasts."

His room, stripped of everything that made it his, looked like nobody had ever lived there. Like we'd imagined the whole thing. The marks on the walls, the worn patches on the carpet, the stains we'd never speak of. Evidence of a life that was already becoming history.

I stood in the doorway for a moment, looking at the empty space. So many late nights, early mornings and everything in between. All of it was reduced to bare walls and bad carpet.

"You coming?" Doyle called from outside.

I turned away. There was nothing left to see.

The drive to Greenway Parkway took less than fifteen minutes. I followed Doyle's Dodge through streets I knew by heart, watching his stuff bounce in the bed of the truck. Boxes, bags and the stereo wrapped in blankets like a baby. Tara was in the passenger seat, probably talking about where everything would go, how they'd set up the new place. Planning the future while I trailed behind.

It wasn't far. That was the thing. Fifteen minutes from the apartment we shared to the apartment he'd share with her. Close enough to visit, far enough to be a different world.

I thought about all the drives we'd taken together. To the bars, to work, to nowhere in particular. The Dodge leading and my Mustang following, or the other way around. Two Roberts on the road, going somewhere, going anywhere. This drive felt different. This one had a destination.

The apartment complex came into view and I understood immediately why Doyle had been so excited. This was nicer than anywhere I'd ever lived. Nicer than anywhere anyone I knew had lived. It had a gated entry, manicured landscaping, the kind of cars in the lot that cost more than I made in a year. It was a different world, just like I'd thought. Doyle's Dodge looked out of place here and so did I.

The apartment itself was everything Doyle had promised. He gave me the tour like he was showing off a mansion. Every room, every feature, every detail that made it better than the place we'd left behind. The kitchen with its granite counters and stainless-steel appliances. The living room with its big windows that looked out over the courtyard. The bathroom with tiles that actually matched and a shower that didn't make weird noises. The bedroom where he and Tara would sleep, already half-arranged in her mind.

The place still smelled new. Like fresh paint, clean carpet and possibility. No beer stains or cigarette smoke soaked into the walls. No history at all. A blank slate for whatever they wanted to build.

Tara was walking through the rooms too, touching surfaces, opening closets. You could see her thinking about furniture, about curtains, about colors and layouts and all the things that would make this space theirs. She had plans... She always had plans.

"What do you think?" Doyle asked.

"It's nice."

"Nice? Hanson, it's perfect. Wait till you see the pool."

He was proud of himself... Genuinely proud. This was his future taking shape, and he wanted me to see it. Maybe he wanted my approval or he just wanted to share the moment with someone who'd been there for the journey.

I walked through the rooms and tried to picture him here. Doyle in this clean, modern space. Doyle with the granite counters and the big windows and the girlfriend who'd made it all happen. He'd come a long way from the guy who couldn't keep a bathroom habitable.

"It's good," I said. "Really. You did good."

He grinned. "Come on... Pool time."

The pool was everything and nothing like I expected. We walked down from the apartment, through a courtyard with more landscaping than some parks, and there it was. The thing Doyle couldn't stop talking about. The beach.

They'd brought in actual sand. Not just around the edges, but a whole section designed to look like you'd walked onto a shoreline. The sand was soft under my feet, white and warm from the sun. Palm trees lined the perimeter. Cabanas with curtains offered shade. Lounge chairs arranged in perfect rows. The pool itself sparkled blue, impossibly clean, the kind of water you see in advertisements.

Doyle stood there taking it in like he was seeing it for the first time. Maybe he was. Maybe every time was the first time for something this good.

"Can you imagine?" he said. "Living here? Having this?"

"It's something."

"Something? Hanson, look at this. We're gonna have people over all the time. Pool parties and barbecues. The whole setup. This is it, man. This is the life!"

He walked toward the water, and I followed. The shallow end had a gradual slope, the sand meeting the water like a real beach. You could walk in slowly, feel the water rise up your legs, ease into it without jumping. Doyle loved that part. He stood at the edge, looking down at where the sand disappeared into blue.

"It's like walking into the ocean," he said. "That's what sold me. That right there."

I looked at the pool. The sand. The shallow end with its gentle slope. It was beautiful and impressive. Exactly what Doyle deserved after years of questionable apartments and roommates who complained about his bathroom. This was moving up. This was making it.

I didn't know why it made me sad. Something about standing there, watching him plan his future around this pool, made me feel awkward. Maybe it was just the goodbye getting to me. Maybe it was nothing or just a feeling with no name, no reason.

Tara came up beside him, slipped her hand into his. They stood there together, looking at the water. A couple planning their life. The pool parties they'd throw. The weekends they'd spend right here. The future unfolding in front of them like that blue water, clean and endless.

Other residents were around the pool. A couple sunbathing on the far side. Some kids splashing in the deep end while their parents watched. Normal people living normal lives in this little paradise. Doyle would fit in here. He fit in everywhere eventually.

"We could have people over every weekend," Tara said. "Get some drinks, some food. Make it a thing."

"That's what I'm saying." Doyle squeezed her hand. "This is the life, Tara. This is it."

She smiled at him. The smile of someone who'd gotten exactly what she wanted. I couldn't blame her for that either.

"You'll come to the first party, right?" Doyle asked me. "I can't have a pool party without you."

"Wouldn't miss it buddy."

He loved that pool. God, he loved it. You could see it on his face, in the way he stood there and, in the plans, already forming behind his eyes. This was his now. This beautiful, perfect place where he'd build his beautiful, perfect life.

I stood there looking at the shallow end and I felt something I couldn't name. Unease... Dread. Something that didn't belong on a sunny afternoon in paradise. I shook it off... There was nothing to worry about. It was just a pool... water, sand and a friend who'd finally found what he was looking for.

We unloaded everything in the heat of the afternoon. Box after box up, furniture through doorways that weren't quite wide enough, the stereo placed with more care than anything else he owned. Tara directed traffic now, pointing to corners and walls, building the apartment in her mind as we filled it with stuff. This goes here. That goes there. No, not like that. She had a vision, and we were just the muscle making it happen.

The complex had other residents, people who watched us haul boxes from the parking lot with that look you give new neighbors. Sizing us up. Wondering if we'd fit in. The Dodge looked rough next to the BMWs and Lexuses in the lot. We probably looked rough too. Sweaty mechanics hauling furniture into a place that seemed too nice for people like us.

But it was Doyle's place now. His and Tara's. They belonged here, or they would soon enough.

Doyle set up his stereo first. Of course he did. Within twenty minutes of arrival, country music was filling the apartment, singing about somewhere else while we sweated through our shirts. The neighbors would have to get used to that. Doyle wasn't going to change his music for anyone.

I put down the last box and looked around. The place was taking shape. Doyle's things mixed with Tara's plans, the start of something new. There was no couch yet, no furniture in the living room. The old couch was in a dumpster on the other side of town. They'd get new stuff... Better stuff. Stuff without history, without stains, without memories soaked into the fabric.

I helped where I could, moved what needed moving, stayed out of the way when Tara had opinions about placement. The dynamic had shifted and I could feel it.

When the music switched to Chris LeDoux, Doyle caught my eye across the room and grinned. Some things didn't change. Some things were still ours, even in someone else's apartment. "There he is... big and beautiful..." laughing as he said it.

"Whatever Doyle..." as I smiled.

The sun was going down when I finally said goodbye. The apartment was mostly set up, boxes unpacked or at least stacked neatly against walls. The place was starting to look like a home. Tara's touches were already visible. A candle on the counter that smelled like something tropical. Towels in the bathroom that matched. Little things that said this wasn't a bachelor pad anymore. This was something else. Something grown up.

Tara was in the kitchen, putting things in cabinets, already making the space hers. She'd thanked me three times for helping. She wasn't a bad person. She loved Doyle, in her way. She wanted this life with him. I couldn't hold that against her. Doyle walked me to the door.

"Thanks, Hanson. For everything."

"It's just moving. I've moved furniture before."

"Not just today." He looked at me, and something in his eyes was heavier than usual. "Everything."

I didn't know what to say. We had a blast living together with bars, women, late nights and early mornings. We were brothers in everything but blood. What do you say to sum that up? What words cover that much ground? I didn't say anything. Just nodded.

He shook my hand that turned into a quick hug. Doyle wasn't a hugger. In all of that time of friendship, of drunken nights, emotional moments and everything in between, I could count on one hand the times he'd hugged anyone. He was a handshake guy, a shoulder slap guy, a nod across the room guy. But he hugged me there in the doorway of his new apartment, and I knew it meant something.

"You'll come over, right?" he said when he pulled back. "We'll still hang out. This doesn't change anything."

"I know."

"I mean it."

"I know you do."

We both knew it changed everything. But you don't say that out loud. You make promises you hope you can keep, and you pretend the world isn't shifting under your feet. I walked to my car and looked back to see him still in the doorway, watching me go. He raised a hand. I raised one back. Then I got into the Mustang and drove away.

The drive home was quiet. No Dodge to follow. No one was waiting at the other end. Just me, the radio and the streets I knew by heart. The sun had set and the city lights were coming on, Phoenix glittering in the distance like something beautiful and cold.

I drove slower than I needed to. There was no rush to get back to an empty apartment. The radio played something I didn't recognize. I changed the station to a country station, because that's what I was used to. Because that's what would have been playing in the Dodge if I'd been following Doyle somewhere instead of driving alone.

I thought about the time we'd lived together. The parties and the quiet nights. The women and the hangovers. The couch that was rotting in a dumpster now, taking all those memories with it. I thought about the Two Roberts, and how that was over now. How it had been over for a while, really. Tara just made it official.

I thought about the pool. The way Doyle looked at it. The plans he was making. Pool parties, barbecues and a future built around that sparkling blue water. He deserved it. All of it. He'd worked hard and found someone worth having. I was proud of him. I truly was.

I pulled into the parking lot at Greenway and Tatum and sat there for a minute. The apartment was there, waiting. I called out when I got inside. Habit. "Doyle?" Then I laughed in response to the echo.

I walked through the empty rooms. The living room with nothing in it. The kitchen still smelled like old beer. Doyle's room, bare and damaged was somehow smaller without his stuff. The bathroom Tara had cleaned, maybe the only thing he'd left behind.

My bedroom was the only room with anything in it. My bed, my dresser and my clothes in the closet. Everything else was gone. The apartment was just walls and carpet now. Echoes where laughter used to be.

I sat on my bed and listened to the silence. No stereo playing country music. No Doyle banging around in the kitchen. No girls asking to use my bathroom because his was a disaster. No beer can towers being built in the living room. No stories being told about nights that got out of hand.

Just silence. The loudest silence I'd heard in a while.

I'd lived alone before Doyle, before the apartment, before the Two Roberts became a thing. I knew what solitude felt like. But this was different. This was the silence after something ends. The quiet that settles in when the noise you got used to goes away forever.

The apartment felt bigger now. The walls farther apart, the ceiling higher. Like the whole place had expanded to fill the space Doyle left behind. I'd have to find a new roommate eventually. Maybe move somewhere smaller or learn to live with the echoes. For now, I just sat there. Letting the day settle. Letting the goodbye sink in.

I think about that pool sometimes. The sand. The shallow end with its gentle slope. The way he stood there, looking at the water like it was everything he'd ever wanted. The joy on his face. Pure and simple with real emotion.

I didn't know then what that pool would do to him. I didn't know that the thing he loved most about that place would be the thing that destroyed him. I didn't know I'd never be able to look at a pool the same way again. He loved it so much. That's what makes it hard, even now. He finally found something worth loving, a place worth calling home, a future worth building. And that future had a pool. And that pool had a shallow end.

Chapter Nine – The Incident

The weeks after Doyle moved out, I barely saw him. Not because we'd grown apart. Not because he'd forgotten about me. He was just busy with the apartment, with Tara and throwing parties at that pool he loved so much. They'd turned the place into party central. Every weekend, sometimes weeknights too. That pool, that sand, that resort-style setup he couldn't stop talking about. People loved it and they wanted to be there, to be part of whatever Doyle was building. He'd finally found a place worth showing off, and he was showing it off to everyone.

I'd been over a few times. I had seen the crowds around the pool, the drinks flowing, the music playing. It was just a new environment where Doyle was running the show the way he always did, except now he had a backdrop worthy of his performance. The beach, they called it. His beach. His new stage.

But I'd noticed something else too. He was drinking more than usual. Going harder than I'd ever seen him go. Every time I visited, he had a drink in his hand. Every story ended with another round. He was celebrating, I figured. Finally having something worth celebrating. He had arrived at the life he wanted. I didn't think much of it. That was just Doyle. He'd always lived full. Now he had a place that matched his energy.

The night it happened; I was on a date. Some girl I'd met a few weeks earlier. She was nice and pretty while probably being way out of my league for sure. We'd gone out once before, and this was the second time. Dinner at a place I can't remember with conversation I can't recall.

The kind of evening that blurs into all the other evenings like it. She talked about her job. I talked about mine. We found things in common that weren't really that common. We laughed at jokes that weren't really that funny. The whole ritual of two people trying to figure out if they want to see each other again.

I went home alone and so did she. That was the unspoken agreement. It was too early to take it further and too uncertain to push. I lay in bed that night thinking about whether I'd call her again. Probably not. There was nothing wrong with her. There just wasn't anything right either. She'd fade into the long list of women who didn't quite fit, and I'd move on to the next one. The endless search of finding the right puzzle piece to match me.

I fell asleep around midnight. It was a normal night. There was nothing special or memorable. While I was lying in bed thinking about a girl whose name I can't remember, Doyle was diving into the shallow end of his pool. While I was falling asleep, he was being pulled from the water by friends who didn't know what they were doing. While I was dreaming about nothing, his life was ending. Not all at once. It would be a slower more dreadful way... Piece by piece. I didn't know any of that. I slept through the whole thing.

I've pieced together what happened from what people told me later. The fragments, versions and second-hand accounts that never quite match up. Everyone who was there remembers it differently. Everyone has their own version of those last hours before everything changed. Isn't that how all accidents go...

But some parts stay the same. Some parts are consistent enough that

I can see them when I close my eyes. The party crowd all gathered around the pool. And then the foolish behavior… leading up to the dive into the water. Then the horrific reality of the aftermath.

I imagined it so clearly… Another party at Greenway Parkway. Another Saturday night. The usual crowd gathered around the pool, drinks in hand, music playing from speakers someone had set up by the cabanas. Country music, or House Techno booming…

The sand was warm under bare feet. The water lit up from below, that impossible blue that made everything feel like vacation. Palm trees casting shadows in the deck lights. The cabanas with their curtains pulled back, people lounging, laughing, living the life Doyle had worked so hard to build.

Doyle was center of attention, as always. More drunk than usual, which was saying something. He'd been going hard all night. Shots with friends. Beers between shots. The kind of drinking that comes from showing off, from wanting everyone to see how good you have it.

Tara was there with friends from work. People from the bar days. A crowd of faces, some I knew, some I didn't. Everyone was having a good time. Everyone was impressed with the place, with the pool, with Doyle's new life. Nobody saw it coming.

It was late in the night around eleven, maybe later. Doyle decided to jump in the pool. He'd done it so many times already that summer. A hundred times at least. It was his pool… His beach. He knew every inch of it, but he dove into the shallow end. The shallow end he'd loved so much. The gradual slope where sand met water, where you could walk in like you were stepping into the ocean. He'd shown it to me with such pride just weeks ago.

He didn't walk in that night... He dove. The way drunk people dive into pools all over the world every summer weekend. Head first, arms out, expecting the water to catch him.

The water did catch him but it wasn't deep enough. His head hit the bottom. The concrete beneath the blue... beneath the paradise he thought he was building. His neck snapped back. The vertebrae that protected his spinal cord shifted. It became compressed then cracked and broke under the impact. The impact damaging the connection between his brain and his body.

In one second. One stupid drunk second. One dive that looked like every other dive he'd ever made. Everything changed.

They didn't know he was hurt. Not at first. That's the part that haunts me. The part I can't stop thinking about, even now. They thought he'd just knocked himself out. They probably thought he hit his head, swallowed some water and needed to be pulled out. So, they pulled him out.

They didn't support his neck. They didn't know to. They grabbed him under the arms and hauled him out of the pool, his head lolling, his body limp. Just trying to help. Just trying to save their friend. They sat him in a chair because that seemed like the right thing to do.

A deck chair by the pool. They propped him up like that would help, like sitting upright was what he needed. His head fell forward and his body wouldn't cooperate. They tried to hold him up and he fell over.

Out of the chair, onto the deck. His neck twisting, his body crumpling. And still they didn't know... still they thought it was just the alcohol, just a bad hit to the head, just something that would sort itself out. When he lost his bodily functions someone finally called 911. Then the ambulance came. The paramedics stabilized his neck, loaded him onto a stretcher and took him away. By then the damage was done. Maybe twice over.

I think about that sometimes. The friends who pulled him from the water. Who sat him in that chair and then watched him fall. They were trying to help. They didn't know that every movement, every adjustment, every well-meaning gesture might have been making it worse. Moving a spinal injury. The one thing you're never supposed to do.

Nobody teaches you that at parties. Nobody tells you when you're pulling your drunk friend out of a pool that you might be hurting him more... You are trying to save him... and you may be tanked at that time too... WTF are you supposed to do? Stop and think... No one knows that they might be severing what's left of his spinal cord. You just act. You just try to help. You just do what seems right in the moment.

Would it have been different if they'd left him floating? If someone had held his neck still? If they'd waited for the professionals instead of hauling him out and sitting him up? I don't know. Nobody knows. The doctors couldn't say whether the original dive did all the damage or whether the rescue added to it. The spinal cord was damaged either way. The question of when and how much was academic. The result was the same.

They were trying to help. That's the cruelest part. They loved him and they were trying to save him... they might have made it worse. They have to live with that guilt, that wondering, that endless replay of what they should have done differently. I would have to live without being there at all. With sleeping through the whole thing. I'm not sure which is harder. I'm not sure it matters.

The call came on Sunday morning. I was still in bed, a little hungover from the wine at dinner, thinking about nothing in particular. My phone buzzed on the nightstand. A number I recognized. It was Mav, a mutual friend and a guy we partied with on the bar circuit, someone I'd see at Lucky's or Harold's back when we still went to those places.

"Hey. You hear about Doyle?"

"No. What happened?"

"Something happened at the party last night. He's at Banner. You should probably go."

"What'd he do?"

A pause. "I don't know exactly but it sounds bad."

I figured he'd broken his leg. Smacked his head doing something stupid. He probably jumped off a roof, got in a fight or crashed the Dodge into something. The kind of thing Doyle would do. The kind of thing we'd laugh about later, once he healed up.

"I'll head over," I said.

"Yeah. You should."

Something in his voice maybe should have told me. Something in the pause before "bad." But I didn't hear it. I was still thinking about broken bones and funny stories. Still thinking about the jokes I'd make when I saw him. I got up and showered. I took my time; there wasn't any rush. It was just Doyle being Doyle, getting himself into trouble. I'd go visit, give him shit, maybe bring him some food from that burger place he liked.

I didn't know but I should have known something. I should have heard it on that phone call. I should have felt it somehow, but I didn't feel anything. I just drove across town like it was any other Sunday.

Banner Hospital was busy when I got there. Sunday morning at a big hospital. Families visiting. People getting discharged. The ordinary traffic of a place where lives hang in the balance every day. I didn't feel like I was walking into anything special. I was just another visitor, another guy checking on a friend who was now a patient.

I parked in the visitor lot, walked through the automatic doors and approached the desk. The lobby smelled like antiseptic and floor wax. Fluorescent lights hummed overhead. A TV in the corner played news nobody was watching. It was an ordinary Sunday morning errand before I got on with my day.

"I'm here to see Robert Doyle."

The woman at the desk typed something into her computer. Looked at the screen then she looked at me. Something changed in her expression. It was a softening of sorts. A careful neutrality that I didn't recognize for what it was.

"Are you family?"

I found the question odd and I lied in a way... "I'm his brother."

We weren't brothers by blood. But we'd been brothers in every way that counted. The Two Roberts. I figured that was close enough to count.

Something in the way her face read was off. Something I should have read but didn't. She nodded slowly, gave me the floor number, the room number, directions I half-listened to. She told me to take the elevators on the right, down the hall, then left at the nurses' station. I was already thinking about what I'd say when I saw him. I was planning the jokes I'd make about whatever dumb thing he'd done.

The elevator took forever or maybe it didn't. Maybe time was already starting to stretch in that way it does when the world is about to change.

The hallway on his floor was quiet. It was too quiet for a Sunday morning. I passed a nurses' station where someone looked up and then looked away. I passed a waiting area where people sat with the kind of stillness that comes from bad news. I found the room number. The door was partially open. I could hear a machine beeping inside. Slow and steady. The sound of something being monitored. I slowly pushed the door open.

Doyle was in the bed. That was the first thing I saw. Doyle, lying flat, not moving. His eyes were open. His head was in a type of device I would later learn is called a Halo. It holds the head and neck in alignment after a spinal injury. Machines surrounded him. Monitors, tubes and things I didn't have names for. The beeping I'd heard from the hallway was his heartbeat, translated into sound. He was alive but only part of him seemed to be working.

Sylvia was sitting beside the bed. His mother, the nurse. She looked up when I came in, and her face told me everything her son's body couldn't. This wasn't a broken leg. This wasn't something we'd laugh about.

"Robert," she said. My name. His name. The same name, different people. "Sit down."

I didn't sit. I stood there in the doorway, looking at my best friend in that bed. He was looking back at me. His eyes were the same. Brown, sharp, alive. But the rest of him was wrong. The stillness of him. The way nothing below his neck seemed to exist anymore.

"What happened?" My voice sounded like someone else's.

Sylvia stood up and walked toward me. She took my hand in both of hers. A mother's gesture, even though she wasn't my mother.

"There was an accident," she said. "At the pool. He dove in and hit his head."

"Is he going to be okay?"

She didn't answer right away. Behind her, Doyle was still watching me. Still listening. He'd heard all of this before. He was watching me hear it for the first time.

"The injury is to the spinal cord," Sylvia said. "Cervical vertebrae. C4."

I nodded like the words meant something to me.

"That means complete paralysis. Below his chest near his neck." Her voice was steady. The nurse in her, taking over, explaining the diagnosis. "He can breathe on his own, which is good. But he can't move his arms. His legs. His hands. He can't feel anything below the injury."

"But that's... that's temporary, right? There's surgery. Physical therapy. Something."

"We're not sure... It may be permanent, Robert." Her hands tightened on mine. "The spinal cord doesn't heal like other tissue. There's no surgery that can fix this. There's no therapy that will bring it back. This is how it is now. This is how it's going to be until we know for sure."

The words landed like stones in water. Sinking, spreading, sending ripples through everything I thought I knew.

I looked at Doyle. He looked at me. His eyes hadn't changed. The same eyes that had laughed at a thousand jokes, charmed a thousand women, seen a thousand sunrises after nights that went too long. But everything below those eyes was different now. Wrong...

The hands that could fix anything lay motionless on the white sheets. The body that had moved through the world with such easy confidence was just a shape under a thin blanket. The future he'd been building with Tara, in the apartment he loved, by the pool he couldn't stop talking about. All of it seemed gone now.

In one dive... One second of a stupid drunk decision in the shallow end of a pool that he'd stood beside just weeks ago, grinning, planning, dreaming of pool parties and barbecues and the life he was finally going to have. The shock of it. I started to say something, but I didn't know what to say... "I'm sorry," Sylvia said. "I'm so sorry."

I didn't know if she was apologizing to me or to her son or to the universe that had done this to him. Maybe all three.

I cried. That's all I remember doing. Standing there in that hospital room, looking at Doyle in that bed, and crying. Not the kind of crying you can control. Not the kind you can stop or hide or push down until later. The kind that comes from somewhere deep, somewhere you didn't know existed until something reaches in and tears it open. The kind that takes over your body and doesn't let go.

I'd cried before. At funerals. At sad movies. When my grandfather died. But this was different. This was crying for someone who was still alive and looking at me. Still there in that bed, watching me fall apart while he couldn't even wipe his own eyes.

I don't know if I said anything. I don't know if he said anything. I don't know how long I stood there, tears running down my face. Time stopped meaning anything. There was just the beeping of the machines and the sound of my own pathetic sobbing. The silence was everywhere else toward the bed where he lay motionless. The memory is a blur. Shock does that. Grief does that. The moment when your world breaks in half and you can't put the pieces together fast enough to understand what's happening.

I remember his eyes. Looking at me while I fell apart. Brown eyes that had seen everything, done everything, charmed everyone. Now they just watched. He watched me cry and try to process what he was already trying to process. What was he thinking? Was he angry that I was making this about me? Was he glad someone else was feeling even a fraction of what he was feeling? Was he already somewhere else, somewhere I couldn't reach, somewhere none of us would ever be able to follow?

I don't know. I never asked. Some questions don't have answers you want to hear. I wasn't there. That's the thing I keep coming back to, twenty years later. The thing I can't forgive myself for. The thing that sits in my chest like a stone I can't swallow or spit out.

I wasn't there. While Doyle was diving into that pool, I was falling asleep in my apartment nearby. While he was being loaded into an ambulance, Sylvia was getting the call that would destroy her life, I was dreaming about nothing.

If I'd been there, would it have been different? Would I have stopped him from diving? Would I have known to hold his neck still, to not move him, to wait for the paramedics? Or would I have done exactly what his other friends did, pulled him from the water and sat him in a chair?

I don't know. I'll never know. And that not-knowing is its own kind of torture. The girl I was with that night she's become a ghost in my memory. Just the vague outline of someone I was making small talk with while my friend's neck was breaking. That's what I was to Doyle that night. An almost. A not-quite. The friend who almost was there. Who not-quite showed up when it mattered.

Everything that comes after is the fall. The hospital stays. The rehabilitation that wasn't really rehabilitation because there was nothing to rehabilitate. The girlfriend who left. The caretakers who failed him. The facility where he ended up. The end he chose for himself. All of it traces back to that pool. That night of the dive and I wasn't there.

I've carried that for twenty years. I'll carry it for twenty more. For however long I have left. The guilt of absence. The weight of not knowing. The endless loop of what-ifs that never resolve into anything useful.
I should have been there, but I wasn't.

That's the story of that night. The story of how everything changed. The story I've never told anyone until now. The story that divided my life into before and after, into who I was and who I became.

Before that night, I was just a mechanic who got lucky enough to be friends with the most magnetic person I'd ever met. After that night, I was the guy who wasn't there. The one who slept through it. I had this guilt inside that I couldn't come to terms with. I wasn't there and in my simple mind, Doyle paid for it. And in a way I've been paying for it ever since.

Everything that comes next is different. It's darker and harder than I could have imagined. It's what happens when the light goes out and all you're left with is the dark silence and the knowledge that nothing will ever be the same again.

Chapter Ten – The Hospital

The first week was a blur. I went to work and then to the hospital and ended up at home. I didn't sleep, not really. I didn't eat much. I just existed, moving through the motions of a life that didn't feel like mine anymore. I was waiting for someone to tell me this was all a mistake. That they'd run more tests. That they'd found something new. That Doyle would wake up one morning and move his hands and everything would go back to normal. Nobody was going to tell me that.

The hospital became the center of everything. Banner Hospital, spinal injury unit, third floor. I learned the route from the parking lot to his room like I'd learned the route from my apartment to the dealership. Automatic and mindless. It was just another path I walked because I had to.

The room was always the same when I arrived. Machines beeping. Monitors displaying numbers I didn't understand. Doyle in the bed, not moving, sometimes awake, sometimes not. The TV on in the corner, playing shows neither of us watched. The window showing a view he couldn't turn his head far enough to see.

I'd sit in the chair by his bed. Sometimes I'd talk. Sometimes I wouldn't. Sometimes he'd respond while other times he'd just stare at the ceiling like I wasn't there.

The nurses came and went. They checked his vitals. Adjusted his tubes. Moved him slightly to prevent sores from forming. They were efficient and kind and completely inadequate for the scale of what had happened. Nobody was adequate for this... how could they be.

The doctors explained it to him a few days in. Or maybe it was a week. Time had stopped meaning much by then. C4 quadriplegia. A complete spinal cord injury at the fourth cervical vertebra. The words sounded clinical, distant, like they were describing someone else. Someone in a textbook. Not Doyle. Not the guy who could fix anything with those hands.

"The injury is complete," Doyle mimicked what the doctor said. "That means there's no signal getting through below C4."

"So, I can't move my... Arms. Hands. Legs. Nothing below the shoulders. I have some movement in my shoulders and neck. Obviously, I can breathe, which is good. But if I had scored a C3 or above I could have cashed out. They usually need a ventilator."

"Cashed out..." I couldn't believe he said that.

"Relatively speaking I'm here." He looked at me with something like compassion. "I know it doesn't feel that way."

He explained the rest of it in terms I struggled to absorb. No surgery could fix this. The spinal cord doesn't regenerate like other tissue. Once it's damaged, it stays damaged. The paralysis was permanent. The word landed like a hammer. Permanent... Forever... For the rest of his life.

The doctor had listed what Doyle would need. Twenty-four-hour care. Someone to do everything for him. Feeding, bathing, dressing, toileting. The words sounded clinical coming from him. Routine. Like he was reading a grocery list instead of itemizing everything a man would never do for himself again.

He'd need catheters. He'd need to be repositioned every two hours to prevent pressure sores. He'd need respiratory therapy because his diaphragm was weakened. He'd need physical therapy to prevent his muscles from atrophying and his joints from freezing. He'd need someone to do literally everything that a human body does, except think. That part still worked. The cruel joke of it. His mind was perfectly fine, trapped in a body that had become a prison.

He'd struggle to feed himself. Never dress himself. Never use the bathroom alone. Never scratch an itch or hold a cigarette or touch someone's hand. He would never feel the sun on his skin below the neck or feel anything at all. He wouldn't be driving the Honda Prelude he'd just bought or go to another bar anytime soon. He would never dance with another woman or do any of the thousand things he'd done without thinking about them, the things that made up a life.

The man who could fix anything was broken beyond repair. And there was nothing anyone could do about it. I nodded along like I understood. But how do you understand something like that? How do you wrap your mind around the idea that your best friend, the most alive person you've ever known, is now trapped in a body that can't do anything? That the hands that could trace an electrical short like a bloodhound, that made trim work look like art, that built beer can towers and charmed women with a gesture, would never move again? You don't understand. You just learn to live without understanding.

I couldn't stop looking at his hands. They lay on the white hospital sheets, curled slightly inward, still. Not the stillness of rest. The stillness of something broken that would never work again.

Those hands had been Doyle. More than his face, more than his voice, more than anything else about him. The way they moved when he talked. The way they held a cigarette like it was part of his body. The way they could find a problem in a wiring harness that had stumped mechanics with decades more experience. The way they touched things with such casual confidence, like everything in the world was waiting to be fixed.

Now they were just shapes. Meat and bone that used to be capable of miracles.

A therapist came twice a day. A woman with a gentle voice and strong hands. She'd take his arm and move it for him. Bend the elbow. Rotate the wrist. Flex the fingers. Range of motion exercises, she called it. Keeping the joints from freezing up. Preventing contractures.

"We do this twice a day," she explained to me once. "The muscles and tendons want to shorten when they're not being used. If we don't stretch them, his arms will curl up and stay that way."

I watched her work. Moving his arm like it was a piece of equipment. Bending and straightening and rotating. Doyle stared at the ceiling the whole time. He couldn't feel any of it. His arm might as well have belonged to someone else. The guy couldn't scratch his own nose or wipe his own face. He couldn't adjust his own pillow, brush his own hair or do a single thing without someone else's hands doing it for him.

I thought about the Lincoln Town Car. The battery drain that had everyone stumped. The way Doyle had traced it to a pinched wire behind the dash, found it in twenty minutes when Richard had been chasing it for days. The way his fingers moved through those harnesses like they were reading something the rest of us couldn't see. Those same fingers were curled on a hospital bed now, being moved by a stranger, feeling nothing at all.

Sylvia was there constantly. She'd taken leave from her own nursing job to be with her son. She had set up camp in the hospital like she was planning to stay forever. Which maybe she was. Forever was exactly what she was facing. The thing about Sylvia being a nurse was that she understood everything the doctors said. There was no translation needed. No gentle explanations. She knew what C4 meant. She knew the complications, the risks, the future stretching out ahead. She couldn't hide in denial the way the rest of us might have. Her training made that impossible.

I found her in the hallway one afternoon. She was leaning against the wall, eyes closed, looking like she hadn't slept in days. Because she probably hadn't.

"How are you holding up?" I asked. What a stupid question but what else do you say? She opened her eyes and turned her head. She looked at me with that combination of strength and devastation that only a mother can manage.

"He'll need care for the rest of his life," she said. "Twenty-four hours a day. Someone to do everything for him. Everything."

"For how long?"

She didn't answer right away. I could see her doing the math in her head. The nurse in her couldn't help it. She was running the numbers. The complications... The infections. The things that take people like her son.

"It depends on a lot of things," she finally said. "Good care... Avoiding infections and staying healthy."

She didn't say the number. She didn't put a timeline on her son's reduced life expectancy. But I could see her thinking about it. Calculating the years while wondering how many there would be. Wondering what would eventually take him.

"He's strong," I said. It was just another stupid thing, but she nodded anyway.

"He's always been strong." Her voice cracked just a little. "That's what makes this so hard. He's still in there. It's still him. Just... trapped."

She excused herself and went back to his room. I stayed in the hallway for a while, thinking about what she'd said. Trapped... That was the word. Doyle was trapped in a body that had become a prison and there was no escape. At least that's what I thought then.

The visits were the hardest part. I didn't go everyday but I tried to get down there as much as I could. I was struggling with the situation, and I didn't know how to sit with him. I was a fish out of water without any clue of what to do or how to act. I'd show up after work, still smelling like grease and transmission fluid, and sit in the chair by his bed. The same chair every time. The same view of machines and monitors and the man who used to be so animated and we'd talk. Or we wouldn't talk. Both were terrible in different ways.

When we talked, we had to navigate around the elephant in the room. I tried not to mention work because he'd never work again. I avoided mentioning the bars because he'd never go to one again. The list of things we couldn't talk about was longer than the list of things we could.

When we didn't talk, the silence was suffocating. Every beep of the machines. Every squeak of shoes in the hallway. Every breath he took, the breath that was now the most his body could do on its own. The silence said everything we couldn't. "The guys at work say hi," I told him one day.

"Yeah?"

"Richard. Dave and even Pops. They're asking about you."

Silence was his initial response. The TV murmuring in the background.

Some game show neither of us cared about. "Tell them I'm fine."

We both knew it was a lie. We both let it stand. What do you talk about with someone whose entire life has been destroyed? Not the future. He didn't have one. Not really... Not the kind we used to dream about over beers. The girls we'd meet, the bars we'd hit, the lives we'd build. All of that was gone now. It was buried in the shallow end of a pool he'd loved.

So, we talked about nothing. The weather, the hospital food and the nurses. Safe topics that didn't touch the gaping wound in the center of everything. And when we ran out of nothing to talk about, we sat in silence and pretended the TV was interesting.

Sometimes he'd try to be the old Doyle. He would crack a joke and flash that grin. For a second you could almost believe nothing had changed. Then you'd look at his hands lying motionless on the sheets, and the illusion would shatter. The moments of silence got longer as the weeks went on. The jokes were fewer. The old Doyle flickered through sometimes, but less and less. Something was dying in him and I could see it happening. Something more important than his body.

I noticed Tara wasn't there. She'd been around at first. Those first chaotic days when nobody knew what was happening. I'd seen her in the waiting room, crying in the hallway and seen her sitting by his bed holding the hand that couldn't feel her. She'd looked devastated and shell-shocked. Like someone who'd just watched their whole future collapse. For a minute, I'd thought maybe I'd been wrong about her. Maybe she was stronger than I'd given her credit for. Maybe she'd be the one thing that got Doyle through this. But then she started disappearing.

First it was just a day here and there. Then it was more days than not. Then it was excuses. She had to work. She wasn't feeling well. She'd come by later. She'd come by tomorrow. The excuses piled up like empty promises, and the visits became less and less... fewer and further between.

"Tara coming by today?" I asked him once.

His face changed. It instantly closed off. Like a door slamming shut.

"She's busy."

"She should be here, Doyle."

"She's got things to do, Hanson. She can't just sit here all day."

I wanted to say yes, she can. That's exactly what she should do. You'd do it for her. You'd give up everything for her.

But I didn't say any of that. Because there was something in his eyes that told me he knew. He knew she was pulling away. He knew what it meant and he couldn't face it. Not on top of everything else.

After that first week, she was never there when I visited. Not once. I asked about her occasionally, and he always had an excuse. She was busy. She had work. She wasn't feeling well. The excuses got thinner and less convincing, but he kept making them.

I didn't push. What was the point? He was lying in that bed, paralyzed, and the woman he'd been building a life with was somewhere else. Doing something else. Being with someone else, maybe. I didn't know for sure then, but I had suspected.

I walked in on a therapy session once. A different kind. They had him in a chair. Not a wheelchair, it was some kind of specialized equipment that supported his body while they worked on him. A therapist was moving his arm through its range of motion while another adjusted something on the chair.

He was just staring at the ceiling. Like he wasn't even in the room. Like his body was a thing that existed separately from him, being manipulated by strangers, feeling nothing.

"We do this twice a day," one of them said to me. "Keeps the joints from freezing. Maintains what muscle tone we can."

Maintains... Like he was a piece of equipment that needed maintenance. Which, in a way, he was now. A body that required constant upkeep just to keep from deteriorating further.

He couldn't participate in any of it. He just had to lie there while other people did things to his body. The man who never needed anyone now needed everyone. For everything.

I thought about him at the dealership. The way he'd disappear under a dashboard for hours, coming out only when he'd found the problem. The concentration in his face. The satisfaction when he traced a short to its source. The way his hands moved through wiring harnesses like they were reading braille.

Now his hands were being moved by someone else. His body was being repositioned by strangers. His life was being managed by professionals who'd go home at the end of their shifts to lives that still worked. This was what remained. This was what the pool had left him.

I left the room and stood in the hallway for a while. I couldn't watch anymore. The fluorescent lights hummed overhead. The smell of antiseptic hung in the air. Somewhere down the hall, a machine beeped its steady rhythm. Life support for someone. A mechanical heart keeping someone breathing who couldn't breathe on their own.

At least Doyle could breathe. That was the one thing. His diaphragm still worked, mostly. He didn't need a ventilator to keep him alive. He just needed everything else.

I thought about his bathroom at the apartment. The disaster zone I'd complained about at times. The towels on the floor. The mysterious stains. The toilet seat I refused to touch. How I'd joked that no woman had ever loved him enough to clean it until Tara came along. Now he'd never use a bathroom by himself again. Ever... For the rest of his life.

I stood in the hallway one evening, watching a nurse wheel someone past. The patient was old. Much older than Doyle. Hunched in the wheelchair, eyes unfocused, barely present. They were headed somewhere. The cafeteria maybe, another test or just a change of scenery in a life that had become all the same scenery. And I thought it...

The thing I'd been trying not to think since I first walked into that hospital room. The thing that made me a terrible person for even considering. Maybe it would have been better if he'd died. The thought hit me like a punch to the gut. I hated myself immediately. What kind of friend thinks that? What kind of person wishes death on someone they love? But I couldn't unthink it. I couldn't stuff it back into whatever dark corner it had crawled out of.

What Doyle was doing in that room wasn't living... The helplessness. The dependence of it. The slow suffocation of everything that made him who he was. That wasn't life, it was something else. Something worse.

Maybe drowning in that pool would have been kinder. It would have been quick and less painful. It would have been over before he knew what happened. Instead of this this slow-motion torture. This permanent imprisonment in a body that had become a cage. I hated myself for thinking it... Then I thought about it again.

I drove home from the hospital that night with the windows down, letting the warm Arizona air wash over me. Trying to feel something other than the weight pressing down on my chest.

Forever... That was the word that kept echoing in my head. This was his life now. A bed in a room with people doing everything for him.

The dealership would have to replace him. They had probably already started looking for someone new. Some other trim guy learning the bays, learning the shortcuts, taking over the space Doyle used to fill. Life goes on. That's what people say. Like it's a comfort... Like the world continuing to spin is somehow a kindness when yours has stopped.

I thought about Sylvia. The calculations in her eyes. The years she was counting. The complications she was cataloguing. She knew things I didn't want to know. Things about what C4 patients face. The infections, the sores and the respiratory problems. All the ways a body trapped in stillness can fail.

I thought about Tara. Wherever she was. Doing whatever she was doing. Already moving on from the man she'd been building a life with. Was she planning her escape from the wreckage. I thought about Doyle lying in that bed staring at the ceiling. Feeling nothing while thinking thoughts I couldn't imagine. Facing a future I couldn't comprehend.

How does someone survive that? How does someone wake up every morning knowing that nothing will ever change? That today will be like yesterday, and tomorrow will be like today, and every day after that will be the same helpless, dependent, imprisoned existence? Knowing that you're trapped in a body that used to take you everywhere and now takes you nowhere?

I didn't know how anyone could survive that. I was starting to wonder if Doyle was asking himself the same thing. Everyone kept saying he was lucky to be alive. The doctors said it. The nurses said it. Visitors said it, the few who came. Lucky... Like survival was automatically a blessing. Like breathing was enough. I didn't think lucky was the right word. I wasn't sure Doyle thought so either.

Chapter Eleven – Tara Unravels

She tried. I'll give her that much. For a little while, she tried. Those first days after the accident, Tara was there. I'd walk into Doyle's hospital room and find her sitting by the bed, holding his hand. The hand that couldn't feel her touch. She'd be crying sometimes and other times just staring at him with this look on her face like she was watching something precious slip away.

I remember thinking maybe I'd been wrong about her. Maybe she was stronger than I'd given her credit for. Maybe she loved him enough to stay. But even then, if I'm being honest, there were cracks.

She couldn't look at him for long. Her eyes would drift to the window, the TV or anywhere else. When the doctors came in to talk about his condition, she'd find a reason to step out. She was going to get coffee. She needed air or she was making a phone call. She always came back, but it took longer each time.

The first week she was there every day. The second week was every other day. By the third week, people started noticing her absence more than her presence.

She showed up. That counted for something but showing up isn't the same as being there. It just looks like it from the outside. I watched her during those early visits. The way she'd hold his hand but keep glancing at the door. The way she'd tell him everything would be okay, but her voice sounded hollow. Rehearsed... Like she was reading lines from a script she didn't believe in.

Once I caught her looking at his hands. Those hands that used to do everything. They were just lying there on the sheets, curled slightly, still. And the expression on her face. It wasn't grief or sadness. It was something else that looked a lot like calculation.

I told myself I was imagining it and she was processing... just struggling like the rest of us. But some part of me knew. Some part of me had always known.

The excuses started small... Work was crazy. She wasn't feeling well. She'd come tomorrow. She was just there yesterday. The avoidance was becoming practiced, rolling off her tongue in a soothing wave. I stopped asking Doyle about her after a while. Every time I did, his face would change. This wall would come down behind his eyes, and he'd defend her like she was the one who needed protecting.

"She's busy," he'd say. "She can't just sit here all day."

"Uh ok..."

"Don't." His voice flat. "Just don't."

So, I didn't. I stopped asking but I didn't stop noticing. She was never there when I visited. Not once after those first couple weeks. I'd casually ask the nurses, casual if Tara had been by today. They'd exchange looks. The kind of looks that said everything without saying anything.

Doyle kept defending her. That was the hardest part. Lying there in that bed, paralyzed from the neck down, and he was making excuses for the woman who was supposed to love him.

"She has her own life," he'd say. "She has things going on."

The desperation in his voice killed me. He needed to believe it. He needed to believe she was coming back, that she was just busy, that everything would be fine once he got out of the hospital. The alternative was too much. On top of everything else, it was just too much. So, he lied to himself and I let him. The visits I did see her at became shorter and shorter. She'd show up for twenty minutes, maybe thirty. Sit by his bed making small talk about nothing. The weather or what was on TV but hardly anything real. There was never anything about the future life they were supposed to have or what happened next. Then she'd check her phone, say she had to go, and disappear for days.

I guess I was on the fence about her perspective. Should she just tell him goodbye and leave it at that.... Or was what she doing a kind mercy of slowing slipping away. I don't know and if I was in her position, I wouldn't know what to do either.

I found out about the money from Sylvia. She pulled me aside in the hallway one afternoon. That tired look on her face, the one she'd been wearing since the accident. It had deepened into something else... Worry. Real worry, "Robert, his accounts..." She hesitated. "The money's running low."

"How? He's been in the hospital for weeks. What's he spending it on?"

She didn't answer right away. She just looked at me with those nurse's eyes that had seen too much. "She has access," Sylvia finally said. "She's been using it."

I felt my body tighten. "Using it for what?"

"I have no idea... maybe things that aren't rent." She shook her head. "I shouldn't be telling you this. It's not my place but someone needs to know. Someone needs to do something."

Doyle had some savings, not a fortune, but enough. Money he'd put away working all those hours at the dealership. The apartment rent was still due every month along with the utilities. His car payment on the Prelude. All of it still going out while he lay in that bed unable to sign a check, swipe a card or do anything except exist.

And Tara had access to all of it. She'd been living with him before the accident. He'd given her his bank card for groceries, for bills, for the normal things couples share when they're building a life together. Why wouldn't he? He trusted her.

Now it looked like she was spending his money on herself. His savings were draining away while he couldn't spend a dime on anything that mattered. While he couldn't spend anything at all.

I thought about saying something to her. Confronting her about the spending. But what would I say? What could I prove? She was his girlfriend. She lived in his apartment. She had access to his accounts because he'd trusted her. Legally, probably, there was nothing wrong with what she was doing. She was just taking care of things while he was in the hospital. Someone had to pay the bills right?

That's what she'd say. That's what she'd tell herself. Taking care of things while managing his affairs. She was being responsible. Meanwhile, the balance dropped lower every week. The savings he'd worked so hard for. The money that was supposed to be their future. All of it was disappearing into some black hole while he lay in that bed with nothing.

Then there was the car. Doyle had bought the Honda Prelude just a few weeks before the accident. He traded in the Dodge for it. That old truck with the hay still in the bed, the one that was so completely him was now gone. He exchanged it for something sleek and new. Something grown-up. He'd been so proud of it. I remember him showing it to me in the parking lot at work. Running his hand along the hood. Talking about the engine, the handling, the way it cornered. A real car... Not a truck for hauling hay and working ranches. A car for the life he was building with Tara. A grown-up car for his grown-up life. Now she was driving it around like it belonged to her.

I heard it first from someone at work. Dave mentioned seeing a Honda Prelude at the mall. Dark color, nice shape. "Isn't that Doyle's car?" he asked. "I saw some woman driving it."

Some woman. Like Doyle didn't exist... Like the car had never been his. Then I heard it again. A friend of a friend mentioning "Tara's Prelude." Tara's. Not Doyle's. Uh... messed up. Hers...

She was most likely telling people it was her car. Driving it everywhere. Shopping and going to the bars. Wherever else she went that wasn't the hospital. He'd traded all of that in for her. For the future they were building together. He thought he needed a grown-up life with the grown-up car and the apartment with the pool. And now it seemed like she was pretending that car belonged to her.

There was a moment when everything changed. I wasn't there for it, but Sylvia told me about it later. The doctors had called a meeting. Tara and Sylvia were there. They were going to discuss Doyle's prognosis. His future and what came next. The doctor laid it out plain, how else could he but be brutally honest. No surgery could help and little would restore function. The spinal cord doesn't regenerate. This was permanent.

Sylvia said Tara's face changed when she heard that word, permanent.

"Something closed off," Sylvia told me. "I was watching her. I couldn't help it. And when he said permanent, something just... shut down behind her eyes."

I knew exactly what Sylvia meant. That calculating look I'd always sensed in Tara. The smart, careful part of her that was always doing the math. She'd been doing it right there in that room. Adding up the years. The decades. The lifetime of caring for a man who couldn't care for himself. A life with things missing... no children or traveling and she'd decided it wasn't worth it. Who could blame her... we were all so young.

After that meeting, the visits dropped too almost nothing. She stopped calling Sylvia to check in. She stopped asking about his progress. There was no progress to ask about. There never would be. She'd made her choice. She just hadn't told anyone yet. Sylvia saw it too. She'd been watching Tara from the moment she started coming around. Mother's instinct, maybe or a nurse's instinct. She knew something was off long before the rest of us.

"I don't trust her," Sylvia told me once in the hallway where Doyle couldn't hear. "I never have."

"She's his girlfriend," I said. Like that meant something.

"She's a survivor," Sylvia said. "And survivors don't stick around for sinking ships."

I wanted to argue but I couldn't. Because Sylvia was right. I'd seen it from the beginning. I just hadn't wanted to believe it. I was clueless in the ways of adulthood at times.

The rumors started a few days later. Someone saw her at a bar... She wasn't alone. She was with a guy, laughing and flirting. I heard it from a friend of a friend. The way you always hear things like that. Third-hand information that feels too ugly to be made up.

"Isn't that Doyle's girlfriend?" someone had asked. "The one whose boyfriend had the accident?"

"Yeah. That's her."

"Who's the guy?"

Nobody knew him... it was just some guy. Some regular guy who probably had no idea he was with a woman whose boyfriend was lying paralyzed in a hospital across town. I wanted to believe it wasn't true and chalk it up to gossip, to misidentification, to the rumor mill spinning lies the way it does. But I knew her. I'd always known her, even when I was hoping I was wrong.

What was I supposed to do? Confront her? Tell Doyle? He was fighting for his life in that hospital bed. Fighting to breathe, to survive, to find some reason to keep going. And I was supposed to tell him his girlfriend was seeing someone else?

Some truths can wait. This one had to. I started paying attention after that. Watching for signs. Listening for news. Part of me hoped the rumors were wrong. That someone had mistaken her for someone else. That there was an explanation that didn't make her a monster.

But the stories kept coming. Different sources, different bars but the same story. Some people aren't evil, they're just empty. Hollow where the loyalty should be. And when the going gets hard, they fill themselves with whatever's convenient. A new guy and a new life. A new story where they're not the villain. That was Tara. That had always been Tara. I just hadn't wanted to see it. I wasn’t mad at her for doing what she did it was more about not telling him straight up. Looking back, I get it, I really do and I don’t harbor ill intent against her.

The question ate at me for days. Do I tell him? He deserves to know. She's cheating on him. Spending his money and driving his car. Living his life while he can't live any life at all. How do you take that away from someone who's already lost everything else?

I went back and forth. I told myself I'd tell him tomorrow. Then tomorrow would come and I'd see him lying there, staring at the ceiling, asking if Tara had called and I couldn't do it. I couldn't add this to everything else he was carrying. He would ask if I saw her or if she mentioned stopping by...

"She's busy," I'd say. "She'll come when she can."

The lies got easier. That scared me more than anything. How easy it was to look my best friend in the eye and tell him what he needed to hear instead of what was true. I was protecting him. That's what I told myself. Shielding him from a truth that would destroy what was left of him. But maybe I was just a coward. Maybe I just didn't want to be the one to break him.

Every visit to the hospital became its own kind of torture. Sitting by his bed. Listening to him talk about Tara. Watching his face light up when he mentioned her name, when he talked about what they'd do when he got out, when he imagined the future that was never going to happen.

"She's been working a lot," he'd say. "That's why she hasn't been around."

"Yeah," I'd say. "Work's been crazy everywhere."

"She'll come by this weekend. She promised."

She hadn't promised anything. She hadn't talked to him in days. I just nodded and played along with the fiction he needed to believe. The lies stacked up. Each one heavier than the last.

Tara unraveled slowly, not all at once. That would have been cleaner maybe kinder, even. A sharp break instead of this slow rot. She fell apart piece by piece kinda like he would. The visits stopping, the money draining along with the car she drove like it was hers.

I don't think she was evil. That would have made it easier to hate her. She was just weak and couldn't handle the weight of forever or face a lifetime of loving someone who needed everything and could give nothing back.

It was human, understandable, forgivable. I was hoping she was going to handle it another way... How... Hell, I don't know. So, what can I say really. It was what it was...

The hardest part was thinking if Doyle would have done it differently. If it had been her in that bed. If she'd been the one who dove into the shallow end and broke her neck. Would he have been there every day. Would have held her hand and talked to her and never once looked at another woman. Would he have given up everything to take care of her. I wasn't sure... but I had hoped he would but I think it might have become a similar story.

Tara couldn't do it and I get it. She was young and life was calling... By the time I worked up the courage to confront her, there was nothing left to save. She'd already moved on in her way and it was a shit show that had one last act before the curtain came down. Either way I couldn't keep pretending I didn't know. I didn't like lying to Doyle's face every time he asked about her. Something had to break. It might as well be me breaking it.

Chapter Twelve – The Confrontation

I couldn't do it anymore. The watching and waiting. The pretending I didn't know what was happening while Doyle lay in that hospital bed asking about Tara. Every lie I told him felt like another nail in a coffin I was building with my own hands.

She was spending his money. Driving his car. Living in his apartment while seeing another man. And I was sitting in that hospital room, looking my best friend in the eye, telling him she'd come by soon. That she was just busy. That everything was going to be fine.

Something had to give. Something had to break. And if no one else was going to do anything, it had fallen upon me to inform him. I don't remember deciding to go to the apartment. One minute I was driving home from work, and the next I was on Greenway Parkway, pulling into the complex where Doyle was supposed to live his perfect life. The place with the pool and the cabanas and the sand they'd trucked in to make it feel like a beach. The place that had destroyed him.

The Honda Prelude was in the parking lot. It was sitting there in a visitor spot like it belonged to someone just passing through. Like it wasn't the car of a man who would never drive again. I parked and sat there for a minute. My hands were gripping the wheel while my heart pounding so hard I could feel it in my throat. I didn't know what I was going to say. I didn't know what I was going to find. I just knew I couldn't keep doing nothing while his life got picked apart like a carcass.

The pool was visible from where I sat. That pool... Sparkling in the afternoon sun like it was innocent. Like it hadn't taken everything in a stupid party moment. The sand around the edges. The cabanas near the shallow end where Doyle had dove in drunk and happy, thinking he was diving into paradise. I got out of the car and walked toward the building.

Each step felt heavy and wrong. Like I was walking into a place I didn't belong... Which I was. This had never been my home. I'd helped Doyle move in, sat on his couch a few times and used his bathroom once or twice. But this was his place. His and Tara's. I was just a visitor.

Now I was coming to confront the woman who was supposed to love him. The woman who'd promised him a future and was now dismantling it piece by piece while he lay in a hospital bed unable to stop her. I stood outside the apartment door, number 117. At the same door I'd helped carry furniture through the day he moved in. He'd been so happy that day about the future he was building. I knocked... The seconds stretched. I could hear movement inside. Footsteps, following a muffled voice. Then the door opened but it wasn't Tara.

The guy standing in front of me was ordinary. Average height with brown hair. He was wearing T-shirt and jeans, the comfortable kind you wear when you're not expecting company. He looked like he'd been here a while. Like he belonged here but he didn't belong here. "Can I help you?" he asked.

"Is Tara here?"

"Yeah." He looked me up and down. "Who are you?"

"I'm a friend of Robert's."

His face went blank without any recognition. Not even confusion, just nothing. A complete void where the name should have meant something. "Robert?"

He didn't know. She hadn't told him a single thing. I stared at him, this regular guy with his regular face, standing in my best friend's apartment like he had every right to be there. He thought he was dating some single woman with a nice car and a fancy apartment. He had no idea he was standing in a paralyzed man's living room, surrounded by things a paralyzed man had bought for a future he would never have.

The disgust hit me like a wave. It wasn't at him. He was just a pawn and didn't know. Tara had made sure of that. She'd erased Doyle so completely that the man standing in his apartment, most likely sleeping in his bed, using his things, didn't even know he existed. That was the depth of it. That was how far she'd gone. Like Doyle had never been real.

"Yeah," I said. "Robert. The guy whose apartment this is."

Something flickered in his eyes. I think it was uncertainty or maybe he was intimidated by me. I wasn't being friendly to say the least. Either way it was the first crack in whatever story Tara had told him. "I thought..." He stopped. Looked over his shoulder. "Tara?"

She appeared from the hallway. The bedroom, probably. Her hair was different than the last time I'd seen her. Shorter. Like she'd made herself over into someone new. Someone who hadn't spent months with a man who was now lying in a hospital bed unable to move. Her face changed when she saw me. Surprise first, then fear. Then that calculating look I'd always seen behind her eyes, the one Doyle never seemed to notice.

"Hanson." She said my name like it was a disease. "What are you doing here?"

"We need to talk."

"This isn't a good time."

"It's never a good time, Tara. That's kind of the point."

The new guy looked between us. Confused as he was sensing something was wrong but not sure what. The poor bastard had no idea what he'd walked into. "You know this guy?" he asked her.

"He's Robert's friend." She said it carefully. Measuring each word.

"From before."

"Before what?"

"It's complicated."

Everything was complicated now. That was her excuse for everything. Her shield against questions she didn't want to answer. "Why don't you give us a minute," I said to the guy. It wasn't a question.

He looked at Tara. She nodded and something passed between them. Some silent communication that made my stomach turn. They had that already. That couple shorthand. The thing that takes time to build. Time she should have been spending at the hospital or telling Doyle goodbye and that she was moving on... He disappeared into the bedroom and closed the door. Now it was just us. The apartment looked different than I remembered. It was half-empty already with boxes stacked in the corner. There were gaps on the shelves where things used to be. She'd been packing for a while. She was getting ready to leave. This confrontation wasn't interrupting anything. It was just speeding up what was already happening.

Doyle's things were mixed in with the boxes. I could see his boots by the door. His jacket on the coat rack. Little pieces of him scattered around the apartment where he'd never live again. It was a scene from a life interrupted. A life being dismantled. Tara crossed her arms... she was defensive already. The walls were going up before I'd even said anything. "You shouldn't be here," she said.

"Neither should he."

"That's not your business."

"The hell it isn't." I felt the anger rising. The thing I'd been pushing down for weeks, boiling up now that I was standing in front of her. "Doyle is lying in a hospital bed. Paralyzed. And you're here playing house with some guy who doesn't even know he exists."

"You don't understand."

"Then explain it to me." I stepped closer. "Explain how you can spend his money. Drive his car. Live in his apartment with another man. While he lies there asking where you are."

Her brow furrowed. "I tried, Hanson. I really tried. I was there every day at first. I held his hand. I cried. I did everything I was supposed to do."

"Supposed to do? He's your boyfriend. Not a chore."

"You don't know what it's like." Her voice cracked with anger or grief, I couldn't tell. Maybe both. "Watching him like that. Knowing it's never going to get better. Knowing he's going to be like that forever. I can't... I can't do this. I'm not strong enough."

"So, you just leave? Take his things and go? Why didn't you tell him?"

"I'm not a bad person."

The words hit me like a slap. I'm not a bad person. Like saying it made it true. Like the words could erase what she was doing. What she'd already done. "Keep telling yourself that."

"You don't get to judge me." She was crying now. Tears running down her face. But her voice was steady and practiced. Like she'd had this argument in her head a hundred times. "You don't know what it's like to watch someone you love disappear. To hold their hand and know they can't feel it. To talk to them and wonder if they're even still in there."

"He's still in there, Tara. He's still Doyle. He's still the guy you said you loved."

"I know." Her voice dropped. "That's what makes it so hard. If he was gone, if he was just... But ... when I'm there. He's watching me and I can see in his eyes that he knows. He knows I can't do this."

"You need to tell him...," I said. "Don't make me do it!"

That landed. I saw it hit her. The truth of it. The cruelty of what she was doing. For a second, something flickered across her face. Shame, maybe or just the recognition of being caught. But she didn't change her mind. I could see it in her face. The decision had already been made. This conversation, this confrontation, it was just noise. Background static to a choice she'd made weeks ago. Maybe the day the doctor said "permanent." Maybe before that. Maybe she'd been planning her exit since the moment she saw him in that hospital bed. "He said he didn't care... I'm not a bad person," she said again. Quieter this time. Like a prayer. Like a plea. Like if she said it enough times, it would become true. "You keep saying that."

"Because it's true. I didn't plan this. I didn't want this. It just... happened."

"Things don't just happen, Tara. You make choices. Every day you don't go to the hospital is a choice. Every dollar you spend of his money is a choice. Every night you spend with that guy in there is a choice."

"I'm not perfect. I never said I was perfect."

"He didn't need perfect. He just needed you to show up or tell him goodbye. This in between slow dying act is cruel."

She didn't have an answer for that. She just stood there, arms still crossed, tears drying on her cheeks. The silence stretched between us like a chasm. I wanted to tell her that bad people never think they're bad. That's what makes them so dangerous. But what was the point? She'd already chosen herself. Nothing I said was going to change that. She'd made her peace with what she was doing. She convinced herself it was okay... she built a whole narrative where she was the victim and Doyle was just some burden she'd had to escape.

The new guy came back out while we were standing there in silence. "Everything okay?" he asked. Looking at Tara. Ignoring me.

"Fine." She wiped her eyes. She put on a smile that didn't reach anywhere real. "Actually, I think you should go. I was going to start packing anyway."

"Packing?" I asked.

"I'm moving out." She said to me. "We talked about it. I can't stay here anymore. Too many memories."

Too many memories. Like Doyle was already dead. Like he was just a ghost haunting this apartment instead of a living person lying in a hospital bed waiting for her. "I'll help you pack," the new guy said. And they started packing. I stood there and watched them. I watched her grab boxes from somewhere as he helped her fold clothes. "You're taking his stuff...," I said.

"We bought it together. He doesn't care, ask him yourself."

"Really..."

She didn't answer, she Just kept packing. The kitchen stuff. The decorations. A lamp he'd picked out himself. Things he'd worked for. The things he'd bought for the future they were supposed to have. All of it was going into boxes. All of it being claimed by someone who was walking away. "He can't even fight you for them," I said. "You know that, right?

He's lying in a bed. He can't sign a complaint, testify or do anything. He doesn't even know you're doing this."

"Yes, he does... he knows." She wouldn't look at me. "...and I know."

"And you're going to take them anyway."

"We bought them together. Most of them."

She kept packing. What could she say? The new guy kept packing. Oblivious. He was a helpful tool in a theft he didn't even know was happening. I almost felt sorry for him. He thought he was helping his girlfriend move. He had no idea he was carrying a dying man's belongings out to his girlfriend's new life. I watched him wrap a picture frame in newspaper. It was one of Doyle's pictures. Something he'd had for years. Some rodeo shot from back in his riding days. The new guy handled it carefully, like it was precious. Like it meant something. And it did mean something... not to him or her. Only to the man who would never see it again.

I couldn't watch anymore. The rage was too much mixed in with the grief. The helplessness of standing there while everything Doyle had built got boxed up and carried away. If I stayed another minute, I was going to do something I'd regret. Say something... Hit something... Break something. Maybe all three. I walked out without saying goodbye. The pool was there on my way to the parking lot. That dam pool. I stood there for a second, staring at the shallow end. The place where he'd dove in. The place where everything ended. The sand was still there. The stupid sand they'd trucked in to make it feel like a beach. Doyle loved that sand. He thought it was the greatest thing in the world. "Can you imagine?" he'd said. "Living here? Having this?"

I could imagine now. I could imagine him lying on a lounge chair, beer in hand, watching the sunset. I could imagine him and Tara out here on summer evenings, swimming and laughing while being young in love. I could imagine the future he'd been building, the life he'd wanted so badly. None of it would ever happen. The pool had seen to that. And now Tara was inside, packing up what was left, erasing the last traces of the man who'd loved this place. I turned away from the water and walked to my car. Then I sat there for a little bit, hands on the wheel, not going anywhere.

I sat in the hospital parking lot that evening. I was trying to convince myself to go in. I couldn't face Doyle, look him in the eye and pretend I didn't know what I knew. The confrontation hadn't accomplished anything. Tara was still leaving. She was still taking his things. She was still with the new guy, building a new life while Doyle's life collapsed around him. All I'd done was watch. All I'd done was say words that bounced off her like rain on a windshield. You can't fight someone who's already surrendered. She'd made her choice weeks ago. The confrontation was me needing to feel like I was doing something... to feel like I was fighting for him. But some battles can't be won. I went in eventually. I sat in the chair by his bed like I always did. After a while the question came up... "How's Tara?" he asked.

The question I'd been dreading. The question that came every time now, more desperate with each asking. His eyes searching my face for something to hold onto. "She's good." The lie came easier than it should have. "She's been busy."

"She hasn't come by in a while."

"She will. She just has a lot going on."

He nodded. He wanted to believe it. God, he wanted to believe it so badly. And I let him. Because the truth would break him. Because he had enough to deal with. Because I was a coward who couldn't stand to be the one who destroyed his last hope. "Tell her I miss her," he said. "Next time you see her."

"I will."

Another lie. The lies were piling up now. They were building a wall between us. Every time I sat in that chair and told him she was busy, told him she'd come soon, told him everything was fine, I added another brick to that wall. Sooner or later, the wall would be too high to see over. Too thick to break through. I was trying to protect him. That's what I kept telling myself. But protection built on lies isn't protection. It's just delay. Just pushing the pain down the road, letting it compound, letting it grow until the reckoning comes and it's worse than it would have been if you'd just told the truth from the start.

But how do you tell someone the truth when the truth might kill them? The truth was coming whether I told it or not. Tara would force my hand eventually. Her accusations along with her justifications. The story she was already telling people about why she had to leave. Word would get back to him one way or another. Through Sylvia or someone at the hospital. Through the universe's cruel habit of making sure people learn the things that hurt them most. It was just a matter of time.

I confronted her because I had to do something. Because I needed to feel like I was fighting for him when he couldn't fight for himself. But you can't save someone from a person who's already decided to leave. You can't protect someone from abandonment that's already happened.

The confrontation changed nothing. All it did was show me how completely she'd moved on. How quickly life can change...

She packed up his life in boxes that day. She took his things, his furniture and his electronics. Pieces of the future he'd been building. And there was nothing I could do to stop her. Nothing legal, anyway. They weren't married. They'd been living together, sharing expenses, sharing a life. It was her word against his, and he wasn't available to even say a word.

That was the cruelest part, maybe. Not just that she was leaving. Not just that she was taking his things. But that he was completely powerless to stop her. He couldn't lift a finger or even make a phone call. He couldn't do anything a person normally does when someone steals from them. He was helpless in every way a person can be helpless.

And she knew it. That's what made it difficult for me. She knew exactly how vulnerable he was, and she took advantage of it anyway. The truth was coming. I could feel it building. The weight of everything I knew, pressing against the walls I'd built to contain it. Every lie was a crack in those walls. Every time I sat by his bed and told him Tara was busy, the cracks spread a little wider. But not yet. Not while he was still in that hospital. Not while he was still fighting to survive. Not while hope was the only thing keeping him breathing. The lies would hold a little longer. They had to. That was all he had left.

Chapter Thirteen - The Truth

The hospital room looked the same as always. The same machines and the same bed with the fluorescent lights buzzing overhead. The smell of antiseptic and something else underneath. Something that smelled like giving up but Doyle looked different.

He was thinner than he'd been a week ago and paler. The muscles in his face had started to go slack in ways they hadn't before. His cheekbones stood out sharper. The hollows under his eyes were deeper. Something fading behind those eyes that I didn't want to name. The visits had become harder. Not just for me but for both of us. There was a weight in the room now. A tension that hung between us like smoke.

His arms lay at his sides, positioned by nurses who came in every few hours to move him. Positioned like he was a mannequin in a store window. The hands that used to fix everything, the hands that could rewire a Lincoln Town Car or gentle a spooked horse, lay useless on the white sheets. They were always still now.

He was watching me differently that day. I noticed it the moment I walked in. His eyes tracked me as I crossed to the chair. Studied me as I sat down. Like he was waiting for something. Like he'd been rehearsing this conversation in his head. I knew what was coming. I'd been dreading it for weeks. "How's work?" he asked. Trying to start with something normal. Something safe.

"Fine."

One word. That was all I gave him. Usually, he'd ask about the dealership. Ask about Pops. Ask about anything to fill the silence. But not today. Today he just watched me. I shifted in the chair and then cleared my throat. I looked at the TV mounted on the wall. Some talk show was on. The sound was off. "You want me to turn that up?"

"No."

The silence stretched. I could feel it coming. Feel the question building behind his eyes. The one he'd been asking for weeks, the one I'd been dodging every time. "Where's Tara?"

There it was. His voice was flat and hard. It wasn't the hopeful tone he'd used before. Something had shifted. "She's been busy," I started. The lie I'd told a hundred times. "She's going to..."

"Stop."

I stopped. "Don't tell me she's busy." His eyes were locked on mine. "Don't tell me she's coming. Don't give me that bullshit, Hanson. Not anymore."

"Doyle..."

"Stop lying to me." The words came out sharp. Edged. "I'm paralyzed, not stupid. She hasn't called. She hasn't visited in weeks. And every time I ask, you look at the floor and change the subject. So, tell me the truth. Where is she?"

I couldn't meet his eyes. I looked at the monitor instead. The steady rhythm of his heartbeat. The only part of him still working like it should.

"I see you," he said. "Every time you come here. You can't look at me when you talk about her. You fidget. You clear your throat. You're the worst liar I've ever known, Hanson. Always have been. You would be a shitty poker player."

He was right. I was a terrible liar. I had always been and he knew me too well to miss it. "Just tell me." His voice cracked. Just slightly.

"Whatever it is. Just say it. I need to know."

I looked at him lying there. My best friend. The guy who'd been my brother and now I had to break his heart. The lies were the easy way out. They'd been protecting both of us. Protecting him from the truth and me from being the one who delivered it. But they were falling apart now. Crumbling under the weight of his questions, his suspicion, his refusal to keep pretending.

I had two choices. Keep lying but the lies weren't holding anymore. He knew something was wrong. He'd keep pushing until the wall collapsed on its own. Or tell the truth but the truth would destroy him. It would take whatever hope he was holding onto and crush it into dust. Neither option was good.

"Doyle..."

"Just say it." He was staring at the ceiling now. Bracing himself. "Whatever it is, just say it."

I took a breath and let it out slowly. I knew I didn't have a choice anymore. The truth was coming out one way or another. Perhaps it was better from me than from someone else. Better from a friend than a stranger. "I went to the apartment," I said. "Last week."

His eyes came back to mine... Waiting. I told him everything. Not all at once but piece by piece. I was trying to be gentle, but there's no gentle way to tell someone their life has been stolen while they couldn't move. The words came out flat. Ugly but true.

"There's someone else." I watched his face. "A guy. He's been at the apartment."

He didn’t respond... Nothing, just his eyes on mine. He wasn’t blinking, he was just waiting for the rest. "He answered the door when I knocked.

He didn't know who I was or who you were. She never told him a thing about you."

Still nothing... But something shifted in his eyes. Something small and terrible. "She's been spending your money. Driving your car around like it's hers. Most likely telling people it's her car."

Still nothing from him. I kept going. "She moved out. Or she's moving out. She was packing when I left. There were boxes everywhere. She was taking your stuff. The TV and the furniture. Whatever she could carry."

His face was going through something. I watched the emotions cross it like clouds moving over a mountain. They resembled confusion at first. Then understanding that was followed by something that looked like pain. But not the pain I expected.

"I confronted her," I said. "I told her what she was doing was wrong. I told her you deserved better. She just kept saying she wasn't a bad person while she kept packing boxes. She said you wouldn’t care about it..."

I waited for the anger and the rage. The betrayal exploding out of him the way it should. He had every right to hate her and curse her name. To want revenge, he'd never be able to get. But that's not what I saw. His face settled into something else. Something quieter... Something that looked almost like... acceptance.

"The new guy," he said. "Does he know? About me?"

"I don’t think so... I’m not sure if she ever told him. He didn't even know your name."

He nodded slowly. Like he was processing each piece, filing it away somewhere deep. I watched his face for anger and betrayal. For some sign that the truth was landing the way it should. "Did he seem nice?"

Doyle said. "The kind of guy she'd like?"

"Doyle..."

"Was he? Nice, I mean?"

I didn't know what to say to that. The new guy had been ordinary and unremarkable. The kind of person you'd forget five minutes after meeting them, but he'd seemed decent enough. He was confused, but helpful. He was completely unaware that he was standing in a paralyzed man's apartment.

"I don't know," I said. "I guess so."

He nodded again. That same slow nod. Processing.

"Good," he said. "That's good. I want her to be happy."

The words hit me like a punch. He wanted her to be happy. This woman who'd stolen from him, abandoned him, erased him from her life like he'd never existed and he wanted her to be happy.

"And the apartment?"

"She's leaving. Taking everything. I don't know where she's going."

Another nod. The same slow motion with the same distant look. Like he was watching something far away. Something only he could see. I waited for the explosion that never came.

"I don't care."

I stared at him. "What?"

"The money." His voice was thick. Heavy. "The car... The stuff. I don't care about any of it."

"Doyle, she..."

"Let her have it." His eyes were wet now. Tears forming that he couldn't wipe away. "None of that matters now. The TV, the furniture... Let her take it. I don't care."

"After everything she did? After she lied to you, stole from you, abandoned you?"

"I don't care about any of that." His voice cracked and broke open on the words. "I just want to see her. Just once more. Just to tell her..."

He couldn't finish. But I knew what he wanted to tell her. That he loved her. That he forgave her. That he understood.

"You don't understand," he said. "She was... she was the last good thing. Before this. Before the accident. She was the thing I was holding onto. The future I was building. When I close my eyes at night, I don't see the accident. I don't see this room. I see her face. I see the apartment. I see the life we were supposed to have."

"I don’t know what to say?"

"I know." His voice was barely a whisper. "But I can't stop seeing it. I can't stop wanting it. Even now... even knowing everything you just told me. I close my eyes and I see her standing at that kitchen counter, making coffee, laughing at something I said. And I know it's never going to happen. I know she's not coming back. But I can't make myself hate her for it."

" Doyle. She's the one who..."

"I know what she did." The tears were running now. Streaming down his face, pooling in the pillow where he couldn't reach them. "I know she left. I know she took everything. I know she's with someone else. But I don't hate her, Hanson. I can't. I've tried... Lying here at night with nothing to do but think, I've tried to hate her. I tried to feel what you're feeling. But all I feel is... I miss her. That's all. I just miss her."

I stared at him in disbelief. This man who'd been robbed, betrayed and abandoned. His girlfriend had stolen his money, taken his things, moved another man into his apartment while he lay paralyzed in a hospital bed. And all he wanted was to see her face one more time. "If she'd just come," he said. "Just once more. I could tell her I'm not angry. I could tell her it's okay. I could tell her I understood why she left. I just... I need to see her. I need to say goodbye."

My heart broke for him. Right there in that hospital room. Watching him cry for a woman who didn't deserve his tears. Watching him love someone who'd already forgotten him.

"She's not coming back."

It hurt me so bad, but I had to say it. I had to make him understand. The truth was cruel but hope without foundation was crueler.

"She's gone, Doyle. She's moved on. She's not going to call. She's not going to visit. I'm sorry."

"You don't know that."

"I do." I leaned forward. I tried to catch his eyes through the tears. "I saw her face. I watched her pack. She's not coming back for forgiveness. She's not coming back at all."

"Maybe if she knew I wasn't angry..."

"It wouldn't matter. She's already convinced herself she did the right thing. Something happened to her during this too... Something I don't understand and she had to escape."

"But if I could just talk to her..."

"She might... we will have to wait for her to do it on her own."

That was the cruelty of it. The final twist of the knife. He was completely dependent on others for everything now. He couldn't dial a phone or write a letter to say the things he needed to say. If she didn't come to him, he would never see her again. And she wasn't coming.

He didn't argue. He just lay there, staring at the ceiling, tears running down his face that he couldn't wipe away. The silence filled the room like water rising. Cold and heavy and impossible to breathe. I sat there and watched him cry.

The tears ran down his temples, pooling in the pillow. He couldn't wipe them away. He didn't even close his eyes to shut out the fluorescent lights that made everything harsh and real. He just lay there. Feeling his heart break while I watched. What do you do? What do you say?

I wanted to hold his hand, but he couldn't feel it. I'd tried that before, early on. I grabbed his hand and squeezed, trying to tell him I was there. And he'd looked at me with those eyes and said, "I can't feel that, Hanson." Those words broke something in me. So now I didn't try. I just sat there with my hands in my lap while his lay useless on the sheets.

I wanted to tell him everything would be okay, but it wouldn't. I wanted to promise him Tara would change her mind, but she wouldn't. I wanted to fix something, anything, the way he used to fix things. He'd been the one who fixed things. He was always the one who knew what to do when everything else fell apart.

But there was nothing to fix here. Nothing to do but sit there and watch my best friend grieve for a woman who'd thrown him away like he was already gone.

It was another piece of Doyle dying. That's what it felt like. First his body. Then his future. Now his heart. Piece by piece, everything that made him who he was... it was getting stripped away. The last hope was extinguished. The final light was going dark. I thought about all the times I'd seen him bounce back from things. He'd always gotten up and found a way through. That was who he was... Doyle didn't stay down.

But you can't get up when you can't move. You can't fight back when you can't lift your arms. You can't do anything except lie there and take it while the world dismantles you piece by piece. The silence stretched. Minutes or hours, I couldn't tell. Just the sound of the machines. The soft hitch of his breathing. The tears he couldn't stop. Eventually, he spoke.

"Will you try?"

His voice was raw. Stripped down to something bare and broken.

"Will you ask her to come? Just once?"

"Doyle..."

"Tell her I'm not angry." His eyes found mine... Red-rimmed and pleading. "Tell her I forgive her. Tell her I just want to say goodbye. Please, Hanson. Will you try?"

What do you say to that? What can you say? I knew it wouldn't matter. Tara wasn't going to come. She'd made her choice and built her new life. She had convinced herself that leaving was the right thing, the only thing, the thing anyone would have done. She wasn't going to come back now, no matter what I said. No matter what message I delivered. No matter how many times Doyle forgave her.

But how do you deny a man this request? How do you look at your best friend, lying there crying, begging you to deliver one last message to the woman he loves, and tell him no? You don't.... I couldn't and so I started to build another wall of lies.

"I'll try."

The words felt hollow. Another lie dressed up as hope, but I said them anyway. Because he needed to hear them and have something to hold onto. Because in that moment, promising to try was the kindest thing I could do.

"Thank you." His eyes closed. The tears kept coming. "Just... tell her I'm not angry. That's all. Tell her I understand."

I nodded even though he couldn't see it. Even though the nod was for me as much as for him.

I left the hospital as the sun was going down. The parking lot was half-empty. My car sat alone in a row of vacant spaces. I walked to it slowly. Each step heavy with everything I'd just done. I told him the truth because he asked for it. Because he deserved it and the lies weren't holding anymore. I was tired of building walls between us.

But the truth didn't set him free. It just gave him something new to grieve. Another loss to add to the pile. Another piece of his life to mourn.

I stood by my car and watched the sun sink behind the buildings. Orange and red bleeding across the sky. Beautiful, the way Arizona sunsets always are. The kind of thing Doyle used to stop and look at. The kind of thing he used to make me stop and look at too.

"You see that?" he'd say, pointing at the sky. "You can't buy that or earn it. It's just there. Free for anyone who bothers to look."

That was Doyle. Finding beauty in things the rest of us walked past. Stopping to appreciate what everyone else was too busy to see. And now he was lying in a hospital bed, crying for a woman who'd already forgotten him, while the sunset painted the sky outside his window. A window he probably couldn't even see from his bed.

I thought about calling Tara. I thought about tracking her down, wherever she'd gone, and delivering Doyle's message... telling her he forgave her and that he loved her. That he just wanted to say goodbye.

I thought about how that conversation would go. She'd make excuses or tell me it was too hard. I imagined her saying she needed to move on and that seeing him would only make things worse for both of them. Or worse yet, she'd say she was doing him a favor by staying away. A clean break was kindest and that he'd be better off without the reminder of what they'd had. She might even believe it. People can convince themselves of anything when the alternative is looking in the mirror and seeing what they really are doing.

The sun disappeared behind the horizon. The sky went from orange to purple to black. I got in my car and started it up. The flow master mufflers echoing in the empty lot. As I put the car into gear, I said I'd try. I didn't promise him that, because I knew I wasn't going to do it.... I'd never call her or leave a message. I wouldn't bother to track her down. And if I saw her... I would pretend just as much as she would that we didn't know each other... That was the way of things now.

I knew how it would end. She wasn't coming back. She was never coming back. The woman Doyle loved was gone, replaced by someone who packed up his life in boxes and walked away without looking back.

She'd never know he forgave her or hear him say he understood with tears running down his face that he couldn't wipe away. She'd moved on, and moving on meant leaving him behind. Completely and permanently without a backward glance.

And Doyle would wait for her anyway. He'd lie in that hospital bed, hoping she'd change her mind, hoping she'd come through that door one more time and he'd get the chance to say goodbye. Not because he thought it would happen. But because hoping was all he had left and giving up on her meant giving up on the only future he could still imagine.

Because the man who'd never quit anything in his life couldn't quit loving her, even when loving her was the thing that was killing him.

The parking lot was dark now as I pulled away. Another visit done as another truth was delivered. It was another piece of both of us broken off and left behind. I tried to brush it off by thinking she wouldn't even remember his name in a few years, probably. She'd move on to her new life with her new guy in her new apartment, and Doyle would become a story she never told, just like me… The sad one…

Some part of Doyle knew it too. He'd wait for her anyway. Because that's what loyalty looks like when there's nothing else left. Holding on even when there's nothing to hold onto. Loving someone even when they've already let go. That was Doyle. Right to the end he was loyal to people who filled his life, including me.

Chapter Fourteen – The Garage

They discharged him on a Tuesday. The hospital made it sound routine. Paperwork was signed, instructions were given and prescriptions filled. He was going home to recover... The delusion was there was a home waiting for him. Like recovery was something that might actually happen.

But Doyle wasn't going home. He didn't have a home anymore. The apartment on Greenway was gone. Tara had taken what she wanted and the lease had been quietly broken under pending litigation. His things were scattered, stolen or sitting in boxes somewhere he'd never see. The life he'd been building was dismantled and distributed while he lay in a hospital bed unable to stop any of it.

He was going back to his mother's house now. Sylvia and Steve's place in Scottsdale. The only option left when there are no other options.

I wasn't there for the discharge. I heard about it later from Sylvia. She'd coordinated everything. The special medical transport. The manual wheelchair that would get him from place to place until insurance approved something better. The boxes of supplies and equipment that had to travel with him. The medications, catheters and the endless parade of things a C4 quad needs just to survive another day.

Doyle didn't say much during the transfer. Sylvia told me that later too. He just lay there on the gurney, staring at the ceiling of the ambulance, not asking questions or making conversation. He didn't complain or anything. He was just existing while people moved him from one place to another like furniture being relocated after a sale.

The house in Scottsdale was nice. One of those suburban places with a neat lawn and a two-car garage and neighbors who waved when you drove past. The kind of house that looks normal from the outside. There wasn't any sign that tragedy had moved in. No indication that a twenty-four-year-old man was lying in the garage, paralyzed from the shoulders down, with no future anyone could imagine.

They'd tried the spare bedroom first. Sylvia explained it to me the first time I visited. The room was too small for the body lift. The ceiling was too low and the space was too narrow. You need room to swing someone from a bed to wheelchair, wheelchair to toilet, toilet back to bed. The Hoyer lift has a metal frame that takes up space, and you need clearance on all sides to operate it safely. The spare bedroom didn't have any of that.

The bathroom doorway was too narrow for a wheelchair. They would have had to knock out walls, widen doorframes, lower counters. Major construction that would take months and cost money they didn't have. The garage was the only option that worked. It had the ceiling height for the lift. It had the floor space to maneuver equipment. They'd added a small accessible bathroom in one corner. It was a concrete floor with area rugs thrown over it to make it feel less industrial. A hospital bed in the center of the room with enough space around it for the lift to swing and rotate.

Sylvia walked me through what they'd done. They had placed pictures on the walls and upgraded the lighting. A TV was mounted where Doyle could see it from the bed. A mini-fridge was added in the corner for drinks and snacks. Some curtains hung in places where there were no windows, just to add some color along with some softness to the hard edges.

They'd done their best. You could see the effort in every detail. The thought that had gone into making it feel like a room instead of a garage. But it was still a garage. You could see it in the ceiling. The exposed rafters crossing overhead. The track for the garage door that had been disabled but not removed, still running along the top of the wall. The electrical outlets placed for power tools, not medical equipment. The slight slope of the concrete floor toward a drain that used to catch oil drips and rainwater from wet cars.

You could smell it. Motor oil and dust underneath the disinfectant. Years of automotive fluids soaked into concrete that no amount of cleaning could fully remove. The ghost of cars that had parked here before the space was converted into something else entirely. Something no one had ever planned for.

The garage door itself had been sealed shut. Insulation added. But you could still see where it was, where it used to open onto the driveway. Now it was just another wall, painted the same color as the others, pretending to be something it wasn't.

"We did what we could," Sylvia said. She wasn't making excuses. She was stating facts.

"You did good," I told her. "It looks nice."

We both knew I was lying. The body lift dominated the room. A Hoyer lift, they called it. A metal frame on wheels with a hydraulic arm that swung out over the bed. A canvas sling that went under Doyle's body. The mechanism that would lift him, move him, lower him down wherever he needed to go.

Four times a day on average. Bed to wheelchair. Wheelchair to toilet. Toilet back to wheelchair. Wheelchair back to bed. Each transfer took time and effort and precision. One person operating the lift while another guided his body, made sure nothing caught or twisted or got damaged in the process.

Sylvia did most of it alone. The lift hung there even when it wasn't being used. A constant presence. A reminder of what Doyle couldn't do for himself anymore. Which was everything. They'd set up the side door for visitors. Steve had installed a doorbell there, run the wiring himself. Made sure the button was low enough that someone in a wheelchair could reach it if they needed to. That way people could come see Doyle without going through the main house. It was easier access with more privacy. That's how Sylvia explained it.

She was right about both things but it also meant you could visit without ever seeing the rest of their lives. You could come and go through that side door like you were visiting a separate building entirely. Which, in a way, you were.

Steve was there when I first visited. Sylvia's husband. Doyle's stepfather. He shook my hand once. Said hello. Then went back to whatever he'd been doing in the house. That was Steve... Not unfriendly or cold exactly. He was just quiet. He was reserved. A man who didn't say much because he didn't know what to say. Some people aren't built for tragedy. They don't have the words or the instincts or whatever it is that lets other people reach out and connect when everything falls apart. Steve was one of those people. He'd married Sylvia years ago, inherited a stepson he got along with well enough, built a comfortable life in a nice neighborhood. None of that had prepared him for this.

He helped when Sylvia asked. He moved things and he fixed things. He ran errands but he didn't initiate. He didn't sit with Doyle and talk or know how to be in that garage with his stepson lying there unable to move. So, he retreated to what he knew. Work, television and the routine of his own life continuing in the main house while Doyle existed in the garage.

I didn't blame him for it, not really. He wasn't equipped for this situation. Few people are. He showed his care the way some men do. Through action. Through practical contributions. The doorbell he'd installed. The grab bars in the new bathroom. The ramp he'd built over the small step at the side door. He never said much but he did those things.

Sylvia was everywhere. In the garage checking on Doyle. In the kitchen preparing food he could swallow. On the phone with doctors, with insurance companies, with medical supply vendors. Running loads of laundry that never seemed to end. Keeping track of medications. Scheduling appointments. Fighting with bureaucracies that didn't care about her son or his condition or anything except their paperwork and their procedures.

She never stopped moving. I noticed that early on. Every time I visited, she was in motion. Adjusting something, cleaning something or checking on something. Her hands were always busy. Her eyes were always scanning for the next task that needed doing. I think she was afraid if she stopped, she'd fall apart.

The nurse in her knew too much. That was part of the problem. She understood exactly what C4 meant. She understood the pressure sores that would develop if he wasn't turned every two hours. She understood the UTIs that could come from the catheter and that respiratory complications could kill him without warning. She understood all the ways a paralyzed body could fail even when everything was being done right. She couldn't unknow any of it or pretend things might get better. She couldn't hope for recovery when she knew there wasn't any coming.

"How are you holding up?" I asked her once.

She laughed. Not a real laugh. The kind that keeps you from crying.

"I'm fine. I'm handling it. What choice do I have?"

None. That was the answer to everything now. She had no choice. Doyle was her son. This was his life now and she was the one who would keep him alive, day after day, for however long that lasted.

The weight of it was crushing her. I could see it in the dark circles under her eyes. In the way her hands shook when she thought no one was watching. In the edge that had crept into her voice, the tightness that came from holding everything together by force of will.

She needed help... Professional help more than one person could provide. But help costs money, and insurance only covered so much. There were waiting lists, paperwork along with a thousand obstacles between her and any relief. So, she kept going... Because stopping wasn't an option.

I started visiting through the side door. That's what it was there for. Ring the bell and let yourself in. No need to knock on the front door and walk through the living room while feeling like you were intruding on the rest of their lives. The first time I stepped into that garage, it hit me harder than I expected.

The body lift looming over the bed. The concrete floor under the rugs. The smell of motor oil and disinfectant mixing into something that would always remind me of this place. Medical equipment against the walls, monitors and supplies. A wheelchair was folded in the corner for when he was strong enough to sit in it.

And Doyle was lying there in the middle of it all. In a hospital bed, in a converted garage, in his mother's house in Scottsdale.

This was his life now. He looked up when I came in but he didn't smile or say much. He just acknowledged my presence with a slight movement of his head. One of the few movements he could make on his own anymore.

"How you doing, Doyle?"

He looked at me. Those eyes that used to spark with mischief and energy filled with life. Now they were empty... "I'm here," he said.

That was all. I'm here... Like existing was enough. It was all he had left to offer. I sat down in the chair they'd placed beside the bed. The visitors' chair. My chair now, I supposed. The spot where I would sit and try to fill the silence with words that didn't matter about a world he couldn't participate in anymore.

The conversations were harder here than they'd been at the hospital. At Banner there had been activity. Doctors checking in with nurses coming and going. Therapists working on range of motion that would never restore function. Things happening with the illusion of progress, even when there wasn't any.

Here there was just quiet. The hum of equipment. The television playing something neither of us were watching. The sound of Sylvia moving around in the house, taking care of everything that needed taking care of. "You need anything?" I asked. "Anything I can bring you?"

He was quiet for a long time. So long I thought maybe he wasn't going to answer.

"No," he finally said. "There's nothing."

I didn't know if he meant there was nothing he needed. Or nothing left at all. He wasn't Doyle anymore. Not the Doyle I knew. The man who'd taught me how to talk to women and two-step while appreciating a cold beer after a hard day. The man who could fix anything, charm anyone, make every room brighter just by walking into it. That man was gone.

What remained was a body in a bed. Thinner every time I visited. The muscles were wasting away because they had nothing to do anymore. His arms lay at his sides, positioned there by someone else, never moving unless someone else moved them. His shoulders had started to round forward, the muscles that used to hold them back now atrophying into nothing.

His hands had started curling in on themselves. The fingers contracting slowly into permanent positions they would never uncurl from. Contractures, Sylvia called them. The tendons shortening because the muscles never moved. His hands... God, his hands. The hands that had fixed everything and built everything and done everything that made him who he was. Now just lying there, useless, curling into fists he couldn't throw or even open.

Sometimes when I looked at those hands, I had to look away. They were the clearest sign of everything that had been lost. The man who could do anything, reduced to hands that couldn't do a single thing.

He didn’t talk as much now. The old Doyle had never stopped talking. Stories, jokes, observations and questions. He'd been interested in everything, engaged with everyone, curious about the world in a way that made you curious too. Now he answered questions with one or two words. He didn't ask too many of his own. He didn't seem to care about anything happening in the world outside that garage. The world had shrunk down to the size of that converted space, and even that was too much for him to engage with. The depression had settled in. You could see it in his eyes. In the flatness where there used to be light. He'd given up hoping for things to get better because nothing was going to get better. He'd stopped looking forward to visits because what was there to look forward to? More of the same of lying there being fed, bathed and moved around like an object.

He watched TV because there was nothing else to do. He couldn't change the channel himself or adjust the volume. He just watched whatever someone else had turned on until someone else came to change it. Hours of daytime television filling the silence of a converted garage.

"Remember when..." I'd start sometimes. Trying to bring back something good talking about the bars, the girls or the dealership. The nights that had felt like they'd last forever. He'd listen and sometimes almost smile. But then the memory would fade and we'd both be back in that garage, surrounded by medical equipment, sitting in the ruins of the life he'd lost.

Every day was the same. Sylvia would come in around seven. Use the lift to get him up, positioning the sling under his body, attaching the hooks, cranking the hydraulic arm until he swung free of the mattress. Then she'd swing him over to the wheelchair, lower him down, adjust his position. Every movement was careful. Every step practiced. The mechanics of moving a body that couldn't move itself.

Next she would take him to the bathroom they'd built. The daily ritual of bodily functions that someone else had to manage for him. Things no one should have to do for their adult child. Things no adult should have done to them but there was no alternative. His body still worked below the injury. It just didn't tell him when or how.

Then back to bed for bathing. Warm cloths and careful attention to every inch of skin. She would be checking for pressure sores that could develop in hours if he stayed in one position too long. And then checking the catheter site for infections. She was always checking everything because everything could go wrong and his body wouldn't tell him when it did.

Breakfast... Food that was easy to swallow, fed to him one spoonful at a time. Nothing too thick, nothing that required much chewing. Medications. A dozen pills that did a dozen things to keep his body functioning. Blood thinners because he couldn't move enough to prevent clots. Muscle relaxants to prevent spasms. Stool softeners because everything was harder when you couldn't push. More pills to counteract the side effects of the first pills.

Then she'd go. Back to the house to take care of her own life for a few hours that included the laundry along with cleaning. The thousand things that needed doing in any household, plus all the extra things that came with having a paralyzed son in the garage.

And Doyle would lie there. Staring at the television. Staring at the ceiling. Waiting for lunch, which would be the same as breakfast. Waiting for the afternoon repositioning, when Sylvia would come back to turn him so he didn't develop sores on his back. Waiting for dinner, which would be the same as lunch. Waiting for night, when Sylvia would come in one more time to turn him, adjust him, check on him before trying to sleep herself.

Then it would start again. And again. And again. Every day the same with no end in sight. No improvement or milestone to reach. No goal except getting through another day so you could get through the one after that. Maintenance... That's all it was. Maintaining a body that couldn't do anything on its own anymore.

I visited as often as I could. Twice a week at first. Then once a week. Then whenever I could make myself walk through that side door and sit in that chair and watch my best friend disappear a little more each time.

I drove home from one of those visits and couldn't stop thinking about it. The concrete floor with the body lift hanging over the bed. The side door that let you come and go without seeing the rest of the house. The smell that never quite went away. The television playing to no one. Doyle lying there, staring at nothing, answering in monosyllables when he answered at all. They'd done the best they could. The spare room really was too small. The bathroom doorways really were too narrow. The garage was the only space that worked. Practical decisions made for practical reasons. No malice in any of it. Just the cold mathematics of caring for a body that needed more space and equipment than a normal room could provide.

But the best anyone could do still wasn't enough. In the hospital there had been the illusion of progress. Doctors making rounds. Therapists setting goals. The sense that something was happening, even if nothing was actually improving. The structure of a medical facility designed to create hope even where hope didn't exist. Here there was nothing. No doctors checking in. No therapists working toward anything. Just Sylvia doing everything alone while Steve retreated to his routines and Doyle lay in that bed waiting for time to pass.

How long could this go on? How long could Sylvia keep doing this by herself? She was already exhausted. Already cracking under the weight of it. One person couldn't provide round-the-clock care indefinitely. The body would give or the mind... something had to give.

And Doyle. How long could he stand it? Lying there day after day with nothing to do and nothing to hope for. Watching television he couldn't control. Waiting for visits that only reminded him of everything he'd lost. Existing without living. Surviving without any reason to survive.

He was existing. That's the best word for it. Not living or dying, just existing. He was taking up space and using resources. Breathing in and breathing out while the days blurred together into one long stretch of nothing.

The Doyle I'd known would have hated this. He would have raged against it and found some way to fight, to push back, to make something happen. That man had never sat still, never waited for life to come to him, never accepted anything less than what he wanted.

But that man was gone. He was buried somewhere under the paralysis and the depression along with the endless routine of maintenance. What was left didn't fight. It didn't rage or do anything except lie there and let the days pass.

I wondered how long anyone could do that before they decided existing wasn't enough. How many days of staring at the ceiling. How many meals fed to you one spoonful at a time. How many times being lifted, lowered and positioned like a mannequin before the weight of it became unbearable. I didn't know the answer then, but I was about to find out.

Chapter Fifteen – The Gun

I rang the bell and let myself in, same as always. The side door Steve had installed, the button he'd wired low enough for a wheelchair to reach. Not that Doyle would ever be reaching it or ever be doing much of anything on his own again.

The garage looked the same. It smelled the same but the odor of urine was beginning to overpower the motor oil. The disinfectant could only mask so much. The body lift hung over the bed like always. The TV played something neither of us would watch. The rugs on the floor along with the pictures on the walls. All the things they'd done to make it feel less like what it was.

But something was off. I could feel it before he even said a word. There was a weight in the air, a tension I couldn't name. Doyle was looking at me differently than usual. Not the flat, empty stare of recent visits. There was something behind his eyes, something building.

I sat down in the chair beside his bed. The visitor's chair. My chair now. The spot where I came to watch him disappear piece by piece.

"How you doing, Doyle?"

He didn't answer right away. Just looked at me. Then he said something I wasn't expecting.

"Can you do something for me?"

"Sure. What do you need?"

"The bag." He moved his eyes toward the floor. "Under the bed. Can you empty it?"

The catheter bag. I'd never done it before. Sylvia always handled that. The intimate tasks, the degrading necessities of keeping a paralyzed body functioning. But she wasn't here right now. She was in the house doing whatever she did when she wasn't in the garage. And Doyle had been lying there knowing that the bag would fill up, unable to reach it, unable to do anything about it.

I got down on my knees and looked under the bed. The bag was there. Plastic, translucent, full of yellow liquid. Heavy when I touched it. Connected to a tube that disappeared under the sheets, connected to him in a way I didn't want to think about too hard.

"There's a drain valve," he said. His voice was flat. Like he was explaining how to check the oil in a car. "At the bottom. You can empty it into the container by the bathroom."

I found the valve and found the container. I did what needed to be done as the liquid poured out warm through the plastic. I didn't look at it more than I had to or think about what I was doing more than I had to. I just emptied the bag, closed the valve, put the container where it belonged.

Then I went to the small bathroom they'd built in the corner of the garage and washed my hands. I stood there at the sink for a moment, looking at myself in the mirror, trying to figure out what I was feeling.

When I came back to the chair, Doyle wouldn't meet my eyes. He was staring at the ceiling. The silence between us was thick and strange.

"Thanks," he said. Still not looking at me.

"No problem."

But it was a problem. We both knew it. A grown man asking his friend to empty his piss bag because he couldn't reach it himself. Because he couldn't do anything himself. The shame of it hung in the air like smoke.

"This is what I am now."

His voice was different. Not flat anymore with something raw underneath. "A man who can't go to the bathroom on my own. Who can't scratch his own face. Who can't do a single dam thing without someone else doing it for him."

I didn't know what to say. So, I didn't say anything.

"You know what I did today?" He was still staring at the ceiling. "I waited. That's it. That's everything I did. I waited for my mother to come feed me. Then I waited for her to leave. Then I waited for you. And now I'm waiting for her to come back so she can turn me, so I don't get sores on my back. That's my life, Hanson. Waiting for other people to do things I can't do myself."

"Doyle..."

"I can't scratch an itch. I can't wipe my own ass. I can't change the channel on the TV. I lie here and I look at that ceiling, and I count the rafters and I wait. That's it. That's my entire existence now. Waiting..."

Something was building in him. I could see it. The frustration. The despair. All the things he'd been holding in during those quiet, empty visits. It was coming out now. The catheter bag had triggered something. Asking me to do that for him had cracked something open.

"I used to fix things," he said. "Remember? I used to be good at that. Cars, engines and anything electrical. Give me a problem and I'd figure it out. That's who I was. The guy who fixed things."

"You were the best," I said. "Everyone said so."

"Now I can't fix anything. I can't hold a wrench. I can't even turn a screwdriver. I can't do a single useful thing with these hands." He tried to move his fingers. They barely twitched. "These hands used to mean something. Now they're just... there. Attached to arms I can't lift. Connected to a body I can't feel."

The silence stretched. I watched him lying there, staring at the ceiling, breathing slowly and even because that was about all his body could do on its own anymore. Then he spoke again.

"I need you to do something else for me."

"What?"

A long pause. The kind that makes your stomach drop before you even know why.

"I need you to get me a gun."

The words didn't make sense at first. Like he was speaking a language I didn't know. I heard them, but they didn't connect to anything real.

"What?"

"A gun, Hanson. I need a gun."

"Doyle, what are you..."

"I can't live like this." His voice wrecked and stuck on the words. "I can't. I can't do it anymore. I'm a burden. On my mother... Everyone has to take care of me. Everyone has to do things for me. Empty my bag. Feed me. Turn me. Wipe me. And I can't do anything back. I can't give anything back. I'm just taking. Taking and taking and taking until there's nothing left."

"That's not..."

"Help me." He turned his head to look at me. His eyes were wet. Desperate and pleading. "Please, Hanson. Please. Help me end this."

I sat there with my hands gripping the arms of the chair, trying to find words that weren't there. Trying to make sense of what he was asking.

Trying to believe this wasn't happening.

"You don't mean that."

"I mean it."

"A gun? Doyle, you can't be serious. You can't even..." I stopped myself. But not fast enough.

"Can't even what? Pull the trigger?" His voice was bitter now. "You think I don't know that? You think I haven't thought about it? I've had nothing but time to think, Hanson. Every minute of every day, lying here, staring at that ceiling. I've thought about everything. But I can figure out a way to pull that trigger."

"You know you can't..."

"I can hold a knife."

The words stopped me cold.

"With the gloves. The adaptive gloves they gave me to help me grip things." He was staring at the ceiling again. "I've tried it. When no one was here. I can hold a knife. Barely, but I can hold it."

The image hit me. Doyle lying in that bed, alone, experimenting with a knife. Testing what his broken body could still manage. Planning his demise.

"But I can't reach," he said. "The angle's wrong. The femoral artery. It's in my thigh. I know exactly where it is. Sylvia talks to herself when she's working. I've learned things. The femoral artery, the carotid, the radial. Which ones bleed out fastest. Which ones you can reach. Which ones hurt."

He paused and I let that sink in.

"The femoral is the best option. It's the biggest artery I could theoretically reach. It runs right through the thigh. Cut that, and you've got maybe a minute before you pass out. Two or three before it's over. But I can't get to it. My arms don't bend right anymore. The contractures... Even with the gloves holding the knife, I'm not sure I can angle my arm down to my leg. I've tried. Lying here alone, when no one's watching. I've tried. I can probably get my neck but..."

The image was horrible. Doyle lying in that bed, alone, struggling to reach his own thigh with a knife gripped in gloved hands that barely worked. Testing angles. Finding out what his broken body couldn't do. Adding it to the list.

"Doyle..."

"I won't feel it." He said it like it was supposed to help. Like that made it better. "I can't feel anything below my chest. The knife could go in and I wouldn't know except by watching. It would just be like going to sleep. And then I wouldn't have to wake up in this bed again. I wouldn't have to ask someone to empty my bag again. I wouldn't have to lie here counting rafters while I wait for someone to come turn me. I wouldn't have to be a burden anymore."

I tried to argue. I said all the things people say. Things could get better. There might be treatments or new research. You can't just give up. He shot down everyone.

"Nothing's getting better. You know that. I know that. Everyone knows that. This is it. This is my life now. Forever lying in a garage while waiting to die slowly. Waiting for my body to fail one piece at a time. Waiting for my mother to wear herself out taking care of me. Waiting for Steve to finally say what he's been thinking since they brought me here."

"You don't know what Steve thinks."

"I know he didn't want me in his house. I know he wanted the garage for his cars, not his stepson. I know he looks at me like I'm a problem he didn't sign up for." He paused. "And he's right. I am a problem... A problem that's never going away. A problem that just keeps taking and taking."

"That's not true."

"It is true and we both know it. The difference is, I'm the one who has to live it. Or not live it... Exist through it. Day after day after day, with nothing to do and nothing to look forward to and no way out."

His eyes found mine again.

"Except there is a way out. And I'm asking you to help me find it."

"What about your mother?"

It was the only thing I had left. The only card I could play.

"What about her?"

"She's doing everything for you. Everything... Her whole life revolves around keeping you alive. She's exhausted, breaking but she keeps going because she loves you. Because you're her son. And you want to what? Make her find you with a knife in your leg? Make her walk into this garage and see that?"

He was quiet. Something flickered in his eyes. The first crack in his certainty.

"She'd understand," he said. But there was doubt in his voice now. "Eventually. She's a nurse. She knows what this is. She knows I'm already gone. The real me. The person I used to be... He's gone, Hanson. He died in that pool. What's left is just... maintenance. She's maintaining a body that doesn't want to be maintained anymore."

"Would she understand, though? Really? Would she understand finding her son dead? Would she understand that you gave up? That you chose to leave her?"

"She'd..."

"You'd destroy her, Doyle. Whatever's left of her after all this, you'd destroy it. She'd spend the rest of her life wondering what she did wrong. Why she wasn't enough. Why her love couldn't save you. She would blame herself..."

He closed his eyes. Tears leaked from the corners. Running down his temples, pooling in the pillow. Tears he couldn't wipe away. "She's already lost so much," I said. "Don't make her lose this too."

The silence stretched. It was long and heavy already full of everything we couldn't say. Then he opened his eyes and looked at me.

"Will you help me?"

I knew what I had to say. I knew it before he asked. I had known it from the moment he mentioned the gun. But saying it was harder than I expected.

"I can't."

"Can't or won't?"

"Both."

"Hanson..."

"You're asking me to kill my best friend." The words came out harder than I meant them. "My brother. You're asking me to put a knife in your hand or position it against your leg or whatever the hell you're imagining. You're asking me to help you die. And I can't. I can't do that. I can't live with that. I won't be able to look in a mirror for the rest of my life if I do that."

"But I can't live like this..."

"And I can't be the one who helps you stop." I leaned forward. "I'll do anything else for you, Doyle. Anything. I'll empty your bag. I'll feed you. I'll sit here every day if you want. I'll carry whatever you need me to carry. I just carried your piss to the toilet and I'll do it again tomorrow if you need me to. But not this. I can't do this. Please don't ask me to do this...."

The silence that followed was the worst kind. The kind that feels like something dying. Then Doyle spoke and his voice was different. It was ugly and bitter. Full of something I'd never heard from him before.

"So that's it."

"Doyle..."

"That's your answer. You're just going to let me rot here."

"I'm not..."

"Some friend you are." He laughed. A hard, ugly sound. "I asked you for one thing. One thing in my entire life. And you said no."

"I said no because I love you."

"Bullshit." His eyes were hard now. The desperation was replaced by anger. "You said no because you're scared. Because you don't want to feel bad. Because it's easier to let me suffer than to get your hands dirty."

"That's not fair."

"Fair?" He laughed again. "You want to talk about fair? I'm lying in a fucking garage, Hanson. I can't move. I can't feel. I can't do anything except lie here and wait for someone else to take care of me. My girlfriend stole everything I owned and is fucking some other guy. My stepfather wishes I was dead. My mother is killing herself trying to keep me alive. And you want to talk about fair?"

I didn't answer. I couldn't answer.

"Must be nice," he said. His voice was quieter now. Colder. "Having legs that work. Being able to walk out of here whenever you've had enough. You come here and sit in that chair and feel good about yourself for visiting. Look at me, being such a good friend. Visiting my crippled buddy in his garage. Then you go home. You go home, Hanson. To your apartment. Your drive your car... you go to work wrenching and I stay here in this fucking garage. Forever."

He wasn't done.

"You know what I think about when you leave? I think about you driving home. Getting out of your car with legs that work. Walking up stairs. Opening your own door. Getting a beer from the fridge. Sitting on your couch. Changing the channel whenever you want. Taking a piss by yourself. Going to bed when you're tired. All the things you don't even think about. All the things that are just... life. Normal life. And I lie here and I imagine it. Every step. Every movement. Every little thing you get to do that I'll never do again."

His voice cracked.

"Do you know how that feels? To lie here every day imagining the life you used to have? The life everyone else still gets to live? While you wait for someone to come feed you like a baby and empty your piss bag like you're already half dead?"

He was trying to hurt me and it was working. Because everything he said was true. Every word...

"Get out."

Two words. That was all.

"Doyle..."

"Get out. I don't want to see you anymore."

"Please, just..."

"You're not my friend." He was staring at the ceiling again. He wouldn't even look at me. "A friend would help me. You're just someone who visits. Someone who comes here to feel better about himself and then goes home to his real life. Get out."

I stood up. I didn't know what to say. There was nothing to say. The space between us had erupted into a canyon I couldn't cross.

I looked at him one last time. My best friend... My brother. Lying in that bed, staring at the ceiling, tears drying on his face that he couldn't wipe away. The body lift hanging over him. The catheter bag under the bed, empty now because I'd emptied it. The rugs on the concrete. The pictures on the walls. The smell of motor oil and disinfectant and despair.

"I'm sorry," I said.

He didn't answer or move. He didn't acknowledge that I'd spoken at all. I walked to the side door. I let myself out. The bell didn't ring when you left from inside. Just silence. Just the click of the door closing behind me. And him. Lying there. Alone. In a garage that smelled like motor oil and piss... it was the end of everything.

I sat in my car for a long time. I couldn't stop shaking or start the engine. I couldn't do anything except sit there and replay the conversation in my head, over and over, wondering if I'd done the right thing.

He'd asked me for one thing. The only thing he'd ever really needed from me. The only thing that mattered to him anymore. And I'd said no. Maybe that made me a good friend. The kind who doesn't let you give up. The kind who refuses to help you hurt yourself, even when you're begging. Or maybe it made me a coward. The kind who's more worried about his own conscience than his friend's suffering. The kind who walks away when things get too hard, too real and too ugly. I didn't know which one I was. Maybe both. Maybe neither. All I knew was that something had broken between us. Something that might never heal. He'd told me to get out. He told me I wasn't his friend and maybe he was right. Maybe a real friend would have helped him. They would have found a way to give him what he needed, whatever that cost.

But I couldn't do it. I couldn't be the one who helped him die. I couldn't carry that weight for the rest of my life or look at Sylvia knowing what I'd done. I was weak and I couldn't live with myself knowing I'd been the one to end him. Even if he hated me for it. Even if he never spoke to me again. Even if he died in that garage, alone, resenting me with his last breath. I couldn't do it.

I started the car and pulled away from the curb. I left him there in that garage, in that bed, with that bag and that lift. The drive home was a blur. I don't remember the roads or the turns or the traffic lights. Just the shaking in my hands and the echo of his voice in my head. Help me. Please. Help me end this. And then, colder... Get out. You're not my friend.

I thought about all the things I should have said. All the arguments I should have made. All the ways I could have handled it better. But none of them would have changed anything. He'd made up his mind before I walked through that door. He'd been lying there, planning, rehearsing, waiting for me to visit so he could ask. And I'd said no.

I didn't know if I'd ever see him again. I didn't know if he'd let me through that side door the next time I rang the bell. I didn't know if he'd even want me to try. Maybe he was right. Maybe I was just a visitor. Someone who showed up to feel good about himself and then went home to his real life. Maybe that's all I'd ever been.

But I knew one thing. I knew I couldn't help him die. Whatever that made me. Whatever it cost me. Whatever happened next. I'd have to live with that choice and so would he.

Chapter Sixteen – Amy

Weeks went by. Maybe months. I lost track. I didn't go to the garage and I didn't call. I didn't know what I'd say if I did. "Get out" was the last thing he'd said to me. So, I stayed out. I respected his wish, if that's what it was. I told myself I was giving him space and that he needed time. I told myself all the things' people tell themselves when they're too afraid to face what they've broken.

The truth was simpler. I was scared. I was scared to ring that bell and have him refuse to see me. I was scared to walk through that door and find that nothing had changed. Or worse yet hear him ask again for the one thing I couldn't give him. I thought he would find a way sooner or later.

So, I stayed away. I went to work and came home. I watched TV and lived my life, such as it was. All the normal things he'd accused me of. Getting out of my car with legs that work. Opening my own door. Getting a beer from the fridge. All the things he'd never do again.

The guilt ate at me. Every day and night. Every time I did something he couldn't do. I'd catch myself scratching an itch and think of him. Lying there, unable to scratch his own face. I'd walk up the stairs to my apartment and picture him. Counting rafters in a garage ceiling. I'd fall asleep and dream about that conversation. Help me please.... Get out. You're not my friend.

Some nights I'd pick up the phone. Start to dial Sylvia's number. Then put it down. What would I say? How's he doing? Is he still alive? Does he still hate me? The questions didn't have answers I wanted to hear. So, I didn't ask them.

Weeks turned into more weeks. The guilt got worse but the fear got stronger. And I told myself, tomorrow. I'll go tomorrow. I'll check on him tomorrow. I'll make it right tomorrow. Until one day I couldn't stand it anymore. The not-knowing was worse than whatever I might find. Even if he threw me out again. Even if he never spoke to me. I had to know if there was anything left to save.

The drive to Scottsdale felt different this time. It was longer and quieter. The roads were the same but everything else was changed. I didn't know what I was going to say when I got there. I didn't have a speech prepared or an apology rehearsed. I just needed to see him and try. I parked on the street like always. The same spot I'd parked a hundred times before. Back when things were different. The house looked the same. Steve's truck in the driveway. Sylvia's car beside it. The garage in back with the side door facing the street. Everything exactly where it should be but something felt off. I couldn't say what, exactly. Just a stillness in the air. A quiet that didn't belong.

I walked to the side door. The one Steve had installed. The button he'd wired low enough for a wheelchair to reach, even though Doyle would never be reaching it. I pressed the bell and waited. Nothing... I rang again, longer this time. I heard the chime through the door but no answer. I didn't hear the TV sounds and no voice calling out that it was open. There was just silence.

Usually, I could hear something through that door. The TV playing whatever Doyle was watching to pass the time. Sylvia moving around, checking on things. The hum of the A/C... Something. But today there was nothing. I tried the handle... It was locked. I stepped back and looked at the garage. I tried to see through the small window, but the angle was wrong. I walked around to the main part of the house, that unease growing with every step. I rang the front doorbell and waited. I heard footsteps approaching and the door opened.

Sylvia stood there looking at me and that was when I knew something had changed. Not because of what she said, but because of how she looked. The dark circles that had deepened with every visit, the exhaustion that had been eating her alive... something was different. She still looked tired. Still looked sad. But not like before. Not like someone drowning.

"Hanson." She seemed surprised to see me. Not unhappy, but surprised. "I... I tried to call you."

"Call me?"

"He's not here anymore."

The words didn't connect at first. Like she was speaking a different language. Not here anymore. The phrase could mean a lot of things. Most of them bad. I felt my stomach drop.

"What do you mean?"

"He's been moved to a facility." She saw my face and quickly added...

"He's alive. He's okay. But a lot has happened since... since you were here last. Come inside. I need to tell you about Amy."

Her kitchen looked the same with clean counters and the coffee maker along with the pictures on the fridge. All the normal things that made a house feel like a home. But something was different here too. It was lighter somehow. Like a weight had been lifted from the walls themselves. Sylvia poured coffee for both of us. She set my cup on the table, sat down across from me and took a breath like she was steeling herself for something difficult.

"I couldn't do it anymore," she said. "Not alone. After... after whatever happened between you two. He wouldn't talk about it. He just said you weren't coming back, and I couldn't handle it by myself. Twenty-four hours a day, every day, with no help and no end in sight."

She wrapped her hands around her coffee cup. She stared at the steam rising.

"I was breaking, Hanson. Physically and mentally. Steve tried to help where he could, but he didn't know how. And Robert needed things I couldn't give him forever. Professional and consistent care. I'm a nurse, but I'm also his mother. And those two things..." She shook her head. "They don't always fit together the way you'd think."

"So, you hired someone," I said. Already knowing where this was going. Already dreading it.

"I hired someone. An agency sent her. A young woman named Amy." Sylvia's voice hardened on the name. "She had good references and a nice smile. She showed up on time and did the work. She gave me a chance to breathe for the first time in months. I thought... I thought she was an answer to a prayer."

She looked up at me. "She wasn't."

The story came out in pieces. Sylvia telling it slowly, like each word cost her something. The relief she'd felt when Amy arrived. The way things seemed to be getting better. The small signs she'd explained away because she wanted so badly to believe.

"Things started going missing. Small things at first. Cash from my purse. I thought I'd miscounted. A watch that had been Robert's. I figured it got misplaced. Then his radio. The little one I'd put by his bed so he could listen to music. It was gone one day. I told myself maybe it broke and someone threw it out."

She shook her head at her own blindness. "Her eyes sometimes were pinned or glazed. Her bathroom breaks that took too long. I saw the signs. I'm a nurse. I know what addiction looks like, but I wanted her to be okay. I needed her to be okay. So, I didn't look too closely. I didn't ask the questions I should have asked. I... just... let it happen."

"Doyle didn't say anything?"

"He couldn't. He couldn't pick up a phone or point a finger. He just had to lie there and watch while she took whatever she wanted. While she stopped doing the things she was supposed to do." Sylvia's voice caught. "The feeding got irregular. The turning stopped. His medications started coming late or not at all and I didn't know. I didn't know because I was finally sleeping. I was finally taking care of myself for the first time in months. While she was nodding off and my son was..."

She stopped. She couldn't finish.

"What happened?" I asked. Already knowing it was bad and feeling the weight of the guilt, I'd been carrying double.

"I came home early one day. Something felt wrong. I can't explain it. Maternal instinct maybe or just luck. I went to the garage and opened the side door."

Sylvia stared at her coffee. Her hands were shaking slightly.

"She was unconscious. In the chair. The chair where you used to sit. She was slumped over and barely breathing. I could see the needle marks on her arms... Fresh ones. She wasn't asleep, Hanson. She was on heroin. Right there. In my garage just ten feet from my son."

"Holy cow..."

"Robert..." Her voice broke. She took a moment. Started again. "He had sores on his back... Pressure sores. Because she hadn't been turning him. He was dehydrated and hungry. Lying in that bed, staring at me with these eyes... He didn't say anything. He didn't have to. I could see what had happened. How long she'd been neglecting him while I was in the house, trusting her, believing everything was fine."

I thought about Doyle lying there helpless. Watching Amy nod off in the chair, knowing she wasn't going to feed him or turn him or do any of the things keeping him alive. Knowing there was nothing he could do about it.

"What did you do?"

"I called 911 for her. She needed medical attention. Then I called Robert's doctor. I had him come look at the sores. They weren't... they could have been worse. Another day or two and..." She didn't finish that thought. "Amy was gone by that night. I didn't press charges. It would have been too much of a hassle with too much publicity. I just wanted her out of my house and out of his life... Gone."

"I should have been there." The words came out before I could stop them. "I should have been checking on him. Visiting, I could have..."

"You couldn't have stopped it." She looked at me. Her eyes were kind. Kinder than I deserved. "You couldn't have been there all the time. And she was clever about it. She was careful... Until she wasn't."

"But if I hadn't stayed away..."

"You stayed away because Robert told you to. I know my son. I know how he gets when he's hurting. Whatever he said to you, whatever happened between you two... you were respecting his wishes. That's not something to feel guilty about."

But I did feel guilty. I would always feel guilty. Because while I was home sleeping in my own bed, eating my own food and living my own life, he was lying in a garage being neglected by a heroin addict. And I wasn't there... again.

"So, you moved him."

Sylvia nodded. "I couldn't do it alone anymore. And I couldn't trust anyone I hired. Not after Amy. There's a facility. They provide specialized care for adults with severe disabilities. They have a professional staff with systems and oversight. People who are watched. People who can't just..." She waved her hand. "Nod off and leave him to suffer."

"A facility."

"I know what you're thinking. I thought it too. I was failing him and giving up on him. I was sending my son away to strangers because I couldn't handle it." She shook her head. "But that's not what happened. That's not how it turned out at all."

There was something in her voice. Something I hadn't expected. Not defeat. Not resignation. Something almost like... hope.

"What do you mean?"

Sylvia leaned forward. And for the first time since I'd walked in, she almost smiled. "They got him an electric wheelchair."

The words didn't register at first. Electric wheelchair? It sounded so simple. So ordinary. But the way she said it, the way her whole face changed...

"He can drive it himself," she said. "With his arm. There's a control, a joystick kind of thing, and he moves it with his arm."

"He can move?"

"On his own. For the first time since the accident." Sylvia's eyes were wet now, but not with sadness. "He's not stuck in a bed anymore, Hanson. He's not staring at the ceiling, waiting for someone to move him. He can go wherever he wants in that place. The common room. The courtyard. The hallways. He can do it himself."

I tried to picture it. Doyle in a wheelchair. Moving under his own power. Going somewhere because he wanted to go there, not because someone else decided to take him. It seemed impossible. After everything in the garage. "Insurance covered it," Sylvia continued. "The facility has equipment we never could have afforded. Specialists who know what they're doing. And Robert... his quality of life has actually improved. I never thought I'd say that. When I drove away from that place after moving him in, I thought I was abandoning my son. I cried the whole way home. But every time I visit now..."

She shook her head, almost disbelieving.

"He's different. Not happy, exactly. I don't know if he'll ever be happy again. But he's not just existing anymore. He's doing things. Talking to other residents. Going outside when the weather is nice. Making choices about his day, even if they're small choices. And the wheelchair..." She laughed. A real laugh. "He's gotten good at it. The nurses' joke about him speeding through the hallways."

That sounded like Doyle. Even broken, even destroyed he was finding a way to be good at something. Finding a way to move faster than anyone expected.

"So, he's... better?"

"Better than the garage. Better than lying in bed all day waiting for someone to turn him. Better than Amy." She reached across the table and touched my hand. "The facility isn't home. I know that but it's giving him something I never could. Independence and a little bit of control. The ability to go somewhere without asking permission."

She wrote the address on a piece of paper. It was a facility in Phoenix. Name, address, phone number, visiting hours. Her handwriting was neat and precise. A nurse's handwriting.

"Go see him," she said. "Please."

"I don't know if he wants to see me."

"He asked about you."

The words hit me harder than I expected. He asked about me. After everything. After "get out" and "you're not my friend" and all the ugly things we'd said to each other. He'd asked.

"He didn't say much," Sylvia continued. "Just asked if I'd heard from you. He asked how you were doing. He tries to act like he doesn't care, but I know my son. He misses you. Whatever happened between you two... you're still his friend. And he needs friends. People who knew him before. People who remember who he was."

I looked at the address. The black ink on white paper was a bridge to somewhere new. "What if he tells me to leave again?"

"Then you leave and you try again later." She squeezed my hand. "But I don't think he will. I think he's been waiting for you to come back. I think he needs you to come back. He just doesn't know how to ask."

That sounded like Doyle too. Stubborn and proud. Even after everything had been taken from him. He was still too proud to admit he needed help and too proud to reach out first. But he'd asked about me. That was something. Not forgiveness, maybe. But something.

I sat in my car looking at the piece of paper in my hand. The address staring up at me. A facility in Phoenix where Doyle was learning to drive a wheelchair. He was finding some kind of independence in a place full of strangers. Moving under his own power for the first time since that night at the pool and he'd asked about me.

I thought about everything Sylvia had told me about Amy. The neglect, the sores on his back. All of it happening while I stayed away, respecting his wish, protecting my own feelings. But I wasn't there and things went wrong anyway. And now Doyle was somewhere else and a hint of improvement lingered in that moment... The garage had never been right for him. I could see that now. It was a garage. Motor oil and concrete along with the smell of cars. A space converted but never transformed. The body lift hanging over him like a reminder of what he couldn't do. The side door with the bell and all the things they'd added to make it functional without ever making it feel like home.

The facility was different. Professional, clinical but it was also freedom. An electric wheelchair with the ability to go somewhere without asking. That was something. That was more than he'd had in months. He could move again.

I started the car and looked at the address one more time. I read the name of the facility, the street, the cross street. I didn't know what I was going to say when I saw him or if he'd even want to see me. But Sylvia said she thought he was waiting and whatever had broken between us might still be fixed.

Maybe she was right. Maybe there was something left to save. Or maybe I'd drive all the way to Phoenix and find that the wall between us was higher than ever. That the gun conversation had ended something that could never be rebuilt. That the words we'd said to each other in that garage had carved wounds too deep to heal.

I pulled away from the curb. Headed toward the freeway. Toward Phoenix and whatever came next. And for the first time in weeks, maybe months, I felt something that wasn't just guilt. I felt hope. It wasn't much... Just a flicker. The image of Doyle speeding through hallways in an electric wheelchair was nice.

He was still alive, fighting and still finding ways to move forward, even if forward was just a hallway in a facility in Phoenix. If I was lucky, he'd let me be a part of that.

Chapter Seventeen – The Facility

I drove to Phoenix with no idea what I was going to say. The address sat on the passenger seat where I'd left it. Sylvia's handwriting. A facility name. A street. The place where Doyle lived now. I'd rehearsed a dozen speeches in my head during the drive. They were filled with apologies, explanations and defenses. I threw them all out before I parked. Whatever happened when I walked through that door, scripted words weren't going to help.

The gun conversation kept playing in my head. The catheter bag and the knife in his femoral artery. All the ugly things we'd said to each other. Those words had echoed in my skull for months. Every time I'd picked up the phone and put it back down. Every time I'd driven halfway to Scottsdale and turned around.

I didn't know if he'd tell me to leave again but I was done staying away. That hadn't worked. Whatever was waiting for me at the end of this drive, at least I'd know.

The building looked like it was trying to be something it wasn't. Cheerful paint with manicured landscaping. A sign out front with a name that sounded almost pleasant. Desert Vista Care Center... Like a resort, or a retirement community. But you could tell what it was underneath. The wheelchair ramps. The wide automatic doors. The parking spaces marked with blue handicap symbols. This was where people came when there was nowhere else to go. People who couldn't take care of themselves. People who needed someone watching them every hour of every day.

People like Doyle.

I sat in my car for a minute, looking at the building. It was nicer than the garage. That was something. It was cleaner and more professional. Not a converted space with concrete floors and the smell of motor oil. But it was also a facility. A place with schedules, staff and other residents. A place that was never going to feel like home.

I got out of the car and walked across the parking lot. The automatic doors slid open as I approached, and a wave of cool air hit me. Air conditioning and antiseptic. The smell of institutions everywhere.

The lobby had a reception desk and a waiting area with chairs that looked comfortable but probably weren't. A few people sat there. One in a wheelchair. One who looked like she might be visiting someone. A staff member in scrubs walked past with a clipboard. I went to the desk. I gave my name. Said who I was there to see.

"Robert Doyle?" The woman checked a list. "He's in the common room. I'll have Michael take you."

Michael was a young guy in blue scrubs with a friendly smile. He led me down a hallway that was wider than normal hallways. Wide enough for wheelchairs to pass each other. Every door had a number and a name card in a slot. The walls had handrails at hip height. The floor was some kind of industrial tile, easy to clean.

As we walked, I saw people. Some in beds, visible through open doors. Some in wheelchairs, parked in hallways or rolled up to windows. Some were staring at nothing while others were watching TV. Some were just sitting there, existing, waiting for whatever came next.

This was Doyle's world now. These were his neighbors. The thought hit me harder than I expected.

"The common room's just through here," Michael said. He pointed to a set of double doors. "He's usually by the windows this time of day."

I thanked him. I stood there for a moment after he left. My hand on the door, not pushing it open yet... I wasn't ready... Then I pushed.

The common room was larger than I expected. Open space with tables and chairs. A TV in one corner, windows along the far wall, looking out at a courtyard with benches and a few scraggly trees. A handful of residents were scattered around. Some at were at tables with others parked near the TV. And there, by the windows, was Doyle.

He was sitting up. Not lying in a bed. He was in a wheelchair. An electric wheelchair with a motor and controls and a joystick on the armrest. And the chair was red. Bright red... The kind of red you'd see on a sports car or a fire truck. It was unmistakable and impossible to ignore.

His back was to me, but I knew it was him. I'd know him anywhere. The shape of his head. The way he held himself. Even in a wheelchair, even after everything, there was something about the way he occupied space that was uniquely Doyle.

And his hand. His gloved hand. It was resting on the joystick, and it was moving. Just slightly. Small adjustments. Shifting his position. Doing things I hadn't seen him do in months. Doing something on his own.

I stood there for a moment, watching. Trying to process what I was seeing. The last time I'd seen him, he'd been lying in a bed in a garage, unable to do anything without help. Now he was sitting up, in a red wheelchair, moving under his own power.

Something loosened in my chest. Something I hadn't realized was wound so tight. I walked toward him. My footsteps were quiet on the tile floor, but he must have heard something or sensed me. His gloved hand moved on the joystick, and the whole chair rotated in a smooth controlled way. And then he was facing me.

There he was in a red electric wheelchair looking at me with eyes that were a little glassy, a little unfocused. The painkillers, I'd learn later. But still looking at me. Still seeing me.

A beat of silence with the TV murmuring in the background. Other residents were going about their routines. The two of us, facing each other, with months of silence and ugly words between us. Then Doyle spoke. "Took you long enough."

I almost laughed and then almost cried... but I settled for something in between a made a joke.

"Traffic."

"Bullshit." His voice was a little slower than I remembered. A little slurred around the edges. But the words were pure Doyle. "You were scared."

I nodded. No point lying about it. "Yeah. I was."

He looked at me for another moment. Then he did something I wasn't expecting. He smiled. Just a little but it was enough.

"Well. You're here now."

We talked about nothing at first. The safe topics. The food here... His room, the staff, the TV in the corner and how nobody ever changed the channel from game shows. I pulled up a chair and sat beside him, and we felt each other out. We tested the waters to see if there was anything left between us.

The gun conversation hung in the air. The garage. The things we'd said. But neither of us mentioned it. Not yet. There was time for that but first we had to remember how to be in the same room together.

"How's the place?" I asked.

"It's not home." He shrugged. A small movement, mostly in his shoulders. "But it's not the garage either. At least here I can move. I can go somewhere when I want." He patted the armrest of the wheelchair. "And the staff actually know what they're doing. Not like Amy."

Sylvia had told me about Amy. The heroin. The neglect. The sores on his back. Hearing him mention her name so casually, like it was just another thing that had happened to him, made my stomach turn.

"I heard about that. I'm sorry I wasn't..."

"Don't." He cut me off. Not angry but just tired. "We'll get to that. But not yet. First tell me about the dealership. Is Pops still running the show?"

So, I told him about Pops and Dave. Richard was finally retiring. The new guys who didn't know what they were doing. The cars that came through, the problems we solved, the flat rate hours we chased. Normal stuff. Mechanic stuff... The world we'd shared before everything changed.

He listened and asked questions. He laughed at a story about a customer who didn't know how to check his own oil. For a few minutes, it almost felt like before. Like we were back at the apartment, shooting the shit after work, two Roberts against the world. Almost...

"Watch this."

He said it with something in his voice I hadn't heard in a long time. Pride filled with excitement. The old Doyle, peeking through the fog of painkillers and institutional living.

His gloved hand pushed the joystick forward, and the wheelchair moved. Smooth and steady. Then he pulled it back, and it reversed. Then a quick push to the side, and the whole thing spun in a tight circle. Fast. Controlled. Like he'd been doing it his whole life.

"Hot rod red," he said. "That's what I call it."

"Hot rod red?"

"My new race car." He almost smiled again. "Insurance finally came through a few weeks ago. They had other colors.... blue, black and silver. I told them red or nothing. If I'm going to be in this thing, it's going to look good."

After everything, Doyle was finding a way to make something his own. Finding the car guy angle in a piece of medical equipment. "When did you learn to drive it like that?"

"Practice." He moved the chair forward again, then executed another spin. Showing off. "The nurses keep telling me to slow down. They say I'm going to run somebody over, but what are they going to do? Give me a ticket?"

I watched him move the joystick. His hand in the adaptive glove, fingers curled around the knob, wrist and forearm doing the work. It wasn't graceful. You could see the effort it took, the concentration. But it worked. He was moving under his own power. Going where he wanted to go.

"First time in months I can go somewhere just because I want to," he said. "The courtyard, the cafeteria or through the hallway. It's not much. But it's something."

"It's a lot, Doyle."

He looked at me. His eyes were glassy but there was something underneath. Something real.

"Yeah. It is."

"You, okay? You seem..." I trailed off, not sure how to finish.

"Fuzzy?" He nodded. "They've got me on some heavy stuff. For the pain."

"Pain? I thought you couldn't..."

"Feel anything? Yeah, well." He laughed, but there was no humor in it. "Nerve pain, they call it. Phantom sensations. My brain thinks my body is on fire even though I can't feel anything. Go figure... Medical science at its finest."

"Does it help? The medication?"

"It helps me not scream." He paused. "But it makes everything a little fuzzy though. It's hard to think sometimes and hard to remember what I was saying in the middle of saying it. Trade-offs..."

Trade-offs. That word again. Everything in his life was trade-offs now. Pain management versus clarity. Independence versus safety. Living versus... the alternative.

"I'm sorry," I said. Not sure what I was apologizing for. Everything, maybe.

"Don't be. It's just how it is." He moved the chair slightly, adjusting his position. "At least I've got this thing. At least I can move. At least I'm not lying in that garage anymore, staring at the ceiling, waiting for someone to turn me."

The silence stretched. It wasn't uncomfortable, just heavy. We both knew what was coming. What we had to talk about eventually. Doyle spoke first. "I shouldn't have asked you that."

I didn't have to ask what he meant. The gun request in the garage. The worst conversation of our lives.

"Doyle..."

"Let me finish." His eyes found mine. Still glassy, but focused now. Determined. "In the garage. What I asked you to do. All of it... It wasn't fair to put that on you."

"You were hurting. You were..."

"I was drowning." He said it simply. A fact, not an excuse. "That bed. That ceiling. Lying there day after day, unable to do anything, unable to help myself, waiting for my mother to wear herself out trying to keep me alive. I couldn't see any other way out."

He paused. The TV murmured in the background. Someone coughed across the room. "But asking you to help me... that was wrong. You're my friend. My brother. That's not what friends are for. I shouldn't have put that weight on you."

I didn't know what to say. The words I'd rehearsed on the drive, all the apologies and explanations, none of them fit this moment. So, I just said the truth. "I wanted to help you. I just couldn't help you in that way."

"I know." He nodded. "I know that now. It took me a while. It took getting out of that garage..." He gestured at the room around us. "It took all this. But I get it now. You were trying to save my life. Even when I didn't want it saved."

"I stayed away too long."

"Yeah. You did." No accusation in his voice. Just acknowledgment. "But you're here now. That's what matters."

"Are we okay?"

I had to ask. I had to hear him say it. Doyle looked at me for a long moment. The red wheelchair and his gloved hands. The glassy eyes and the slightly slurred speech. All the ways he'd changed since the last time I saw him. All the ways he was still the same.

"We're okay."

Two words... It was simple as that. We're okay after everything and the months of silence. The ugly things we'd said. We're okay.

I felt something relax and subside. It was a tension I'd been carrying since the last time I walked out that garage door. A weight I'd been dragging around without realizing how heavy it was.

"I'm going to come back," I said. "When I can."

"You don't have to..."

"I know I don't have to. I want to."

He didn't say anything but something shifted in his expression. Gratitude maybe or relief. Maybe the simple acknowledgment that he wasn't alone anymore. That someone was going to show up for him. That the brother he'd pushed away had come back.

"Okay then." He moved the chair slightly. A small adjustment. "Every week."

"I'll try but it might be every other week."

I stayed another hour. We talked about nothing important. The facility. The other residents. The shows he'd been watching on the TV in his room and on his mother's visits. About the red wheelchair and how he was already planning modifications, if they'd let him.

"Same motor as the base model," he said. "But I bet I could get ten percent more efficiency if I adjusted the controller. They've got it calibrated for safety, not speed."

"They probably don't want you running people over."

"Their loss."

It was easy. Easier than I'd expected. It wasn't like it was before. We couldn't go back to before. But something new. Something built on top of the wreckage. Two friends, finding their way back to each other.

When it was time to go, I stood up from my chair and looked down at him. Doyle in his hot rod red wheelchair waiting for whatever came next.

"I'll see you next week."

"I'll be here." He said it with just a hint of dark humor. "Not like I've got anywhere else to go."

I laughed and he almost smiled. And for a moment, just a moment, everything was okay.

The drive home was different than the drive there. I left the windows down, letting the desert air blow through the car. The sun was setting over the mountains, painting the sky in shades of orange and red. Hot rod red, I thought. Doyle would appreciate that.

Something had changed. It wasn't fixed. You can't fix what happened to us. But it was mended. Patched good enough to hold the brotherhood that had cracked in that garage, the ugly words and the impossible request, all of it was still there underneath. But we'd built something over it. A bridge... A way forward.

He was still Doyle. Still my brother and still the guy I'd followed through country bars, dealerships and all the time in between. He was just different now. He had a wheelchair instead of legs in a facility instead of apartment. He was on painkillers instead of Jim Beam, but it was still him. He was still the person who'd taught me how to live, even if he was still figuring out how to do it himself.

I thought about what Sylvia had said. His quality of life has improved.

I hadn't believed it at first. How could it improve? He was paralyzed. He was in a facility. He was never going to walk again, never going to work again, never going to be the Doyle who could light up a room just by walking into it.

But I'd seen it today. The wheelchair and the pride in his voice. The way he moved that joystick, showing off, finding joy in something small. Hot rod red... My new race car. The mechanic finding a machine to master, even now. It wasn't much. But it was something and something was more than he'd had in that garage.

I merged onto the freeway, heading back to my apartment. Next week, I'd be back. Because that's what brothers do.

Chapter Eighteen – Decline

I kept my promise. Every other week, sometimes once a week. The drive to Phoenix became routine. I knew which exit to take, which streets to turn on, where to park. The staff at the front desk knew my name. "He's in the courtyard," they'd say. Or "He's in his room today." Or "He's having a rough one." I learned the rhythms of that place. The meal times along with the medication schedules. Which nurses were kind and which ones were just going through the motions. And I watched him, visit by visit, slowly fade.

It didn't happen all at once. That's not how decline works. It's not a cliff you fall off. It's a slope. A gentle, terrible slope that you only notice when you look back and realize how far down you've come. One week he'd be sharp, almost like the old Doyle. The next week he'd be foggy, distant, somewhere I couldn't reach. Good days and bad days. That's what the nurses called it. As if it were that simple.

Some days were better than others. I walked in one afternoon and found him in the common room, in his red wheelchair, actually using it. Moving around. He saw me come through the door and his face lit up in a way it hadn't in weeks. "Hanson. Get over here. I've got something to show you."

I pulled up a chair beside him. He looked more alert than usual. The fog lifted, at least for now. His eyes had some of the old spark. "Watch this," he said.

His gloved hand pushed the joystick, and the wheelchair moved forward. Then back. Then a sharp turn, tighter than I'd seen him manage before. He spun the chair in a full circle, fast, controlled, and came back to face me with something like pride on his face.

"Been practicing," he said. "The nurses keep telling me to slow down. I keep telling them this is hot rod red, not hot rod reasonable."

I laughed. A real laugh. It felt strange coming out of my throat, like I'd forgotten how.

"Still the fastest thing in here," he said. "Some old guy in a manual chair tried to race me down the hallway last week. I beat him by a mile."

"You're racing the other residents?"

"What else am I gonna do?" He almost smiled. "Besides, I won. That's all that matters."

For a moment, just a moment, it was like before. We were back at the dealership, giving each other shit about who could finish a job faster. Like he was still the Doyle who wrench all day and impress the old timers without trying. Then the moment passed and his face changed. The fog started creeping back in around the edges. But at least there was a moment. At least there were still days when I could see him underneath.

The next week was different. I walked in and he was sitting there in the red chair, and his face looked wrong. It took me a second to figure out what had changed. Then I saw it. His cheeks were sunken. His jaw looked different. His whole face had collapsed inward somehow.

"They took my teeth," he said.

I stood there, not knowing what to say. His voice was different too. Softer. Mushier around the consonants. "All of them?"

"All of them." He tried to smile, and it was awful. All I saw was gums where teeth should be. The face of an old man on a twenty-five-year-old body. "Dental problems. I couldn't brush them right or floss. I couldn't do any of the things you're supposed to do to keep your teeth. The infections kept coming back. So, they just..." He made a gesture with his head. "Took them."

"Jesus, Doyle."

"Yeah." He stared at the wall. "I can't even keep my own fucking teeth, Hanson. What's next? What else are they going to take?"

I didn't have an answer. There wasn't one. He'd already lost his legs, his arms, his independence, his girlfriend, his apartment, his future. Now he'd lost his teeth. Another piece of himself carved away. Another indignity in a life that had become nothing but indignities.

"They said I might get dentures," he said. "Eventually. When the gums heal. But for now..." He shook his head. "I look like my grandfather. I'm twenty-five years old and I look like my dead grandfather."

I sat with him for two hours that day. We didn't talk much. Just sat there, him in his red chair, me in the visitor's seat, watching the afternoon light move across the floor. Sometimes, that's all you can do is just be there.

The medications kept multiplying. Every visit, it seemed like there was something new. Something for the pain. Something for the spasms. Something to help him sleep. Something to keep him from getting blood clots. Something for the infections that kept coming back. Something for the depression that was eating him from the inside. Always something...

I saw the nurses with their carts, lined with little cups of pills. Each cup had a name on it. Doyle's cup was always full.

"Pain meds," he explained one day, when I asked. "Nerve pain. Muscle relaxants. Blood thinners. Antibiotics. Stool softeners. Sleeping pills. Something new they're trying for the spasms." He paused, trying to remember. "I think there's more. I lose track."

His eyes were glassier than before. His words came slower. Sometimes he'd start a sentence and forget where he was going with it. The sharp mind that used to solve electrical problems no one else could figure out was dulling. It was blurring and disappearing into a chemical haze.

"I hate these pills," he said. "They make me stupid."

"But they help with the pain?"

"Without them I'm screaming." He looked at me through the fog. "So, pick your poison, right? Pain or stupidity. Those are my choices. Pain or stupidity."

He'd tried to cut back once. He told the nurses he wanted to reduce the dosage. They let him try. Three days later he was begging for them back. The nerve pain, he said, was like being on fire. Like his whole body was burning even though he couldn't feel anything. The contradiction didn't make sense to me. It didn't have to. It was his reality, and it was unbearable. So, he took the pills and he got foggier. And I watched him disappear, one dose at a time.

The wheelchair became harder to use. I noticed it gradually. Some days he'd be in the common room, rolling around, almost like his old self. Other days he'd be in his room, in bed, the red chair sitting empty in the corner.

"My arm's getting worse," he said. "The contractures."

I'd learned what that meant by now. The muscles and tendons

shortening. The joints freezing up. Even with physical therapy, even with the exercises they made him do, his body was curling in on itself. His fingers didn't straighten anymore. His wrist was stuck at an angle. The arm that used to push the joystick with pride now struggled to reach it.

"Can you still use the chair?"

"Some days." He stared at the red machine. Hot rod red... His race car. "Not like before. I used to be able to go anywhere. Now it takes everything I've got just to get to the courtyard. And by the time I get there, I'm too tired to enjoy it."

"Maybe they can adjust the controls. Make it easier."

"Maybe." He didn't sound hopeful. "Or maybe this is just how it goes. You get something good, and then you lose it. Same as everything else."

The independence that the wheelchair had given him, the hope it had represented, was slipping away. The thing that had made him proud, that had let him feel like something other than a patient, was becoming just another reminder of what he couldn't do. Even the red chair couldn't save him. Nothing could.

We talked about the past a lot. The dealership, the bars, the girls and the apartment. The good times, before everything changed.

"Remember that night at Lucky's?" he asked. "With the twins?"

"The ones who thought we were actual brothers?"

"They couldn't believe it. Two Roberts... They kept asking if we were messing with them." He almost laughed. The sound was different without teeth. Softer but sadder. "God, those were good times. The smoke. The music. The way everything felt possible."

"The Two Roberts," I said.

"The Two Roberts." He nodded. "Remember the routine? How we'd introduce ourselves? 'I'm Robert.' 'I'm also Robert.' And they'd look at us like we were crazy, and by then you already knew which one you were going home with."

"It worked every time."

"Almost every time. Remember that girl in Cave Creek? The one who didn't buy it?"

"The one who threw a drink at you?"

"I had it coming." He smiled. Or tried to. "I definitely had it coming."

We'd go like that for hours sometimes. Remember when. Remember Vegas... Swimming in the past because the present was unbearable and the future was too dark to look at. He wanted to go back there, I think. Not physically. That was impossible but in his mind. He wanted to remember who he'd been before the pool took it all away. And I played along. What else could I do? At least in the past, he could still walk.

Not every visit was good. I showed up one afternoon and found him in bed, not the chair. The red wheelchair sat in the corner, unused. He was staring at the ceiling. Wouldn't look at me when I came in.

"Hey, Doyle."

Nothing. I pulled up a chair anyway. I sat down and waited.

"What's the point?" he said finally. Still staring at the ceiling. His voice was flat. Dead.

"What do you mean?"

"All of this. The visits. The pills. The wheelchair I can barely use anymore. What's the point?" He finally looked at me. His eyes were hollow. Empty in a way I hadn't seen since the garage. "I'm just waiting to die in here, Hanson. Every day is the same. Pills... Bed... Chair... Bed... Pills. Over and over until my body finally gives out."

"Doyle..."

"You don't know." His voice sharpened. A flash of anger through the fog. "You can't know. You come here, you sit with me for a few hours, and then you leave. You go back to your life. Your apartment. Your job. Your legs that work. And I stay here. In this room. In this bed. Waiting for nothing."

I didn't argue. I couldn't argue. Everything he said was true.

"I know it's hard," I said. Useless words, but I had to say something.

"Hard." He laughed. A bitter sound. "Hard is working overtime. Hard is paying bills. This isn't hard, Hanson. This is hell. This is a slow-motion hell that never ends."

We sat in silence for a long time. The anger drained out of him. What was left was just exhaustion. Just surrender.

"I'm not good company today," he said finally. "Come back later."

So, I left. I drove home with his words echoing in my head... Waiting to die in a slow-motion hell. And I wondered how many more visits we had. How much longer he could hold on. How much longer he wanted to.

The nurses pulled me aside sometimes. "He's declining," one of them told me. A woman named Patricia, her kind eyes combined with a matter-of-fact voice. "It's common with injuries like his. The body just... breaks down over time. Complications compound the infections along with respiratory problems. The medications help, but they also take a toll."

"How long?" I asked. Not sure I wanted the answer.

She didn't give one. She just shook her head. "It's hard to say. It could be months or years. Every case is different."

"Is there anything..."

"You're doing it." She put a hand on my arm. "Your visits. They matter more than you know. He talks about you. The friend from the dealership. He lights up when he knows you're coming." She paused. "Well. As much as he lights up anymore."

I thanked her. What else could I do? Keep coming and showing up. Keep watching him disappear piece by piece. That was all I had to offer.

"You know why I'm still here?"

He asked it out of nowhere. One of the better days. The fog lifted enough that I could see him underneath. The real Doyle, looking out at me from behind the glassy eyes.

"Why?"

"Because you keep showing up." He said it simply. Like it was obvious. "Because sometimes we talk about the old days and I remember what it felt like to be alive. To be a person. Not a patient... Not a problem but a person."

I didn't know what to say.

"That's all I've got left, Hanson. These visits. These memories. You." He looked at me. Really looked through the painkillers, the exhaustion and all the layers of loss. "You're the only one who remembers who I was. The only one who knew me before. Everyone else just sees this." He gestured at himself in the wheelchair with his gloved hands. The sunken face. "But you remember and when you remember, I can remember too."

The weight of it settled on me. The responsibility. He was holding on because of me because I kept showing up. Because I kept reminding him of the man he used to be. I didn’t believe him fully... I knew other people were still seeing him and that they mattered more than me.

"I'm not going anywhere," I said.

"I know." He nodded. "I know you're not."

I watched him fade. That's the truth of it. Visit by visit, week by week, I watched Doyle disappear. The teeth, the pills and the fog. The stories about the past because the present was unbearable. The good days were getting fewer, and the bad days were getting worse.

Everything that had made him Doyle was being stripped away, piece by piece, until what was left was just a body in a chair, waiting for whatever came next. That's what friendship looks like at the end. Not fixing things. You can't fix this. Just being present. Just staying. Just promising, over and over, that you won't leave. That you'll be there until there's nothing left to be there for.

I drove home from every visit with the weight of it pressing down on me. The memories we'd shared. The laughter that used to come easy and now came hard. The glimpses of the old Doyle that appeared less and less often. The certainty, growing stronger every week, that we were running out of time.

Chapter Nineteen – Remembering

He didn't want to talk about now anymore. Every conversation started the same way. "Remember when." The dealership memories combined with the bars, the girls and the life we'd lived before everything changed. I played along because what else could I do? The past was the only place he wanted to be. The only place where he was still whole.

I knew what he was doing. Even then, I knew. This wasn't just nostalgia. This was a man revisiting his life. Saying goodbye to who he'd been. Every "remember when" was a farewell. Every story was a closing and a part of me understood. "Remember that Lincoln?"

He asked it one afternoon, eyes far away, seeing something from before.

"Which Lincoln?"

"The Town Car. The one with the electrical gremlin no one could figure out." He was smiling. A real smile, or as close as he could manage without teeth. "Everyone had worked on that car. Pops, Allan and even Richard took a crack at it. Nobody could find the problem."

"You spent three hours tracing that wire."

"And I found it." Pride in his voice. Real pride. "It was behind the dash... pinched against the firewall. Three hours, crawling through that wiring harness, testing every connection. Everyone else had given up. But I found it."

"You always found it."

"I was good at that, Hanson." He turned his head to look at me. His eyes were wet. "I was really good at that. The electrical stuff. The trim work. The things nobody else wanted to touch. Pops used to send the hard ones to me. 'Give it to Doyle. He'll figure it out.' And I did. I always did."

"You were the best," I said. "Everyone knew it."

"I could fix anything." His voice cracked on the word. "Anything... Cars that stumped everyone else. Electrical nightmares. Wiring puzzles. Give me a problem and I'd trace it down, find the cause, fix it." He tried to move his hands. They barely twitched inside the gloves. "That's who I was. The guy who fixed things."

He was quiet for a moment. Looking at those hands. Those useless, broken hands. "Now I can't fix anything. I can't even fix myself."

It was an awkward moment and then it was gone as he rushed into another memory... He was repeating himself but I didn't care. I knew he needed this and I enjoyed giving him that happiness even if it was brief.

"Remember Rockin Rodeo?"

Another trip to the past. "That first night you came with me." He was almost laughing. "You were so out of your element. City boy in a country bar. You didn't know how to two-step. You were terrible."

"I was terrible," I admitted.

"But you learned. You got better... And we had some nights, didn't we?" His eyes were far away again. Seeing the smoke and the neon. The girls in their Rockies. The life we'd lived before. "The Two Roberts. Remember the routine? 'I'm Robert.' 'I'm also Robert.' And they'd look at us like we were crazy."

"It worked, though."

"It worked." He shook his head. "Remember that night with the sisters? The ones who didn't believe we weren't actual brothers?"

"They wanted to see our driver's licenses."

"And we showed them. Two Roberts with different last names. They still didn't believe us." He was smiling again, lost in the memory. "We had them going all night. They couldn't decide which one of us was lying."

We sat with that memory for a moment. The smoke surrounding the music. George Strait on the jukebox with longnecks and Jim Beam. The world we'd lived in before everything changed.

"God, I miss it," he said. "The smoke. The music. The way everything felt possible. Like the night could go anywhere. Like anything could happen." He paused. "Nothing feels possible anymore. Nothing feels like anything."

Back into that awkward silence as his mind screamed to catch up and cut through the fog... it was sad to see him fight it when recalling the memories. It was almost as if he was losing access to them in his mind. The pain killers were robbing him of that too as they dulled the pain.

"You know what I miss?"

He said it out of nowhere. I waited.

"Not just the sex. Well, yeah, the sex." He almost smiled. "But not just that. The way they looked at me. Women. The way they used to look at me. Like I was somebody. Like I mattered. Like I was a man."

"You're still..."

"No." He cut me off. Not angry... Just tired. "I'm not. Not to them. Not to anyone. You know how people look at me now? The nurses. The staff. Even my mother. They look at me like a patient. A problem. A thing to take care of... Something to be managed."

I didn't know what to say.

"I used to walk into a bar and women would notice. Not because I was handsome. I wasn't handsome. You were the handsome one. But there was something. A presence... A way of being in the room that made people look." He stared at the ceiling. "Now I roll into a room and people look away. They don't want to see me. They don't want to deal with what I represent."

"Doyle..."

"I miss being wanted, Hanson. I miss being a man." His voice was barely a whisper. "I miss the way Rita used to look at me. The way Casey used to laugh at my jokes. The way any girl at any bar might decide that tonight, I was the one she wanted to go home with. That's gone. That's all gone and it's never coming back."

Then he blanked out... and then as the fog cleared he jumped into another memory.

"I was going to open my own shop someday."

He said it quietly. Almost to himself.

"What?"

"A shop. My own place. Custom electrical work. Specialty stuff. The kind of jobs no one else would take." He was staring at the ceiling. At the future that would never happen. "I had it all figured out. I was gonna start small and build a reputation. I would get the work that the dealerships couldn't handle. The classic cars and the custom builds. The electrical systems no one else understood."

"You would have been good at that."

"I would have been great at it." No arrogance in his voice. Just truth. "I had the skills, the knowledge and the hands." He laughed. A hollow sound now that echoed in his toothless mouth. The hands. God. Everything always came back to the hands.

"What else?" I asked. Because I could tell he wasn't done.

"I don't know. Get married, maybe and have kids. Nothing crazy... just a life. A normal life with work I loved. Someone to come home to and a house with a garage where I could tinker on weekends. A dog, maybe. Kids running around." He paused. "Simple stuff. The stuff everyone takes for granted."

"Doyle..."

"You know what I lost, Hanson?" He turned his head to look at me. His eyes were wet. "Not just my legs. Not just my arms. Not just my hands. I lost every single thing I was going to be. Every version of me that was waiting down the road. The shop owner. The husband. The father. The old man tinkering in his garage. All of them gone... All of it." His voice broke. "Because I dove into a pool."

Five words. Because I dove into a pool. The smallest decision... The stupidest decision. A moment of drunken showing off, and every possible future erased.

He talked about everything again. The dealership. The bars. The girls. Every piece of our shared history. But there was one thing we never talked about. One name that never came up. Tara...

He talked about Rita. He talked about Casey. He talked about the girls at Rockin Rodeo, Lucky's and Harold's, the ones whose names he'd forgotten. But he never mentioned Tara... He would mention the apartment on Greenway Parkway. The pool with the sand that he'd called "the beach." But he would leave out the life they were building together before it all fell apart. None of it. We talked around her like a hole in the floor. Like if we got too close, we'd fall through and never stop falling. Some memories were too heavy to carry. Some betrayals too raw to revisit.

"Do you think about it?"

The question caught me off guard.

"Think about what?"

"The party. The night it happened." He was watching me. "Do you think about it?"

I nodded. "All the time."

"Do you blame yourself? For not being there?"

I couldn't answer. The guilt was too thick in my throat.

"It wasn't your fault, Hanson." His voice was firm. Clear. "It was never your fault. I was drunk. I was showing off. That's who I was. The guy who did stupid shit to make people laugh. You being there wouldn't have changed that. You couldn't have stopped me."

"You don't know that."

"I do know that." He held my eyes. "I've had a lot of time to think about it lying in bed, staring at ceilings. Running through that night a thousand times. And the truth is, I would have done it no matter what. Because I was an idiot. Because I thought I was invincible. Because it never occurred to me that something could go wrong. I could never have imagined something like this..."

He paused and I let that sink in.

"It was never your fault. It was always mine. And I need you to stop carrying that around." His voice softened. "Let it go, Hanson. Please. For me."

I knew what he was doing. All these conversations. All these "remember whens." The dealership memories. The bar memories. The absolution about the night of the accident. Each conversation felt like a chapter being closed. A box being packed up. A room being emptied.

He was wrapping things up. Tying off loose threads. Making peace with everything that had happened. The gun conversation echoed in my head. The garage. "I need you to get me a gun." The desperation in his voice. The knife and the femoral artery. All the ways he'd thought about ending it.

Was this that? Was this him planning something? Was all this nostalgia just preparation for goodbye?

I wanted to ask. The question burned in my throat every visit. "What are you doing, Doyle? What are you planning? Is this goodbye?"

But I couldn't. I was afraid of the answer. Afraid that asking would make it real. So, I just listened, watched and played along with the memories. And wondered how much longer we had.

I drove home after each visit with all of it in my head. Everything he'd been. Everything he'd lost. Everything he was trying to hold onto before it slipped away completely.

I knew what he was doing... The long goodbye. The wrapping up. The slow process of revisiting a life before leaving it behind. I could see it in the way he talked. The finality underneath the nostalgia. The closure in every "remember when."

But I didn't know how to stop it. I didn't know if I should try. He'd asked me once, in that garage, to help him die. I'd said no. I'd walked away and he'd told me I wasn't his friend. Now he was finding his own way. Saying goodbye on his own terms. And there was nothing I could do except sit there and listen. I could remember with him. Hold the memories he was trusting me with. The man who used to light up every room was slowly going dark. And I was watching it happen. Helpless. Heartbroken. Holding onto him with the only thing I had left. The memories of who he used to be.

Chapter Twenty – The Hands

Richard said it first, that day in the shop. Years ago now, when Doyle was just the new trim guy and I was watching him work on a headliner everyone else had given up on. "Those hands of his," Richard said. "God almighty."

I knew what he meant. I'd seen it too. The way Doyle worked was different from everyone else. Faster and more precise. His hands seemed to know what to do before his brain caught up. Like they had their own intelligence and their own memory.

I watched him that day. The way his fingers traced the fabric. The way they found every attachment point. The way they worked the material back into place with a patience and precision that seemed almost inhuman. No wasted motion or hesitation. Just the hands doing what they were born to do.

"Best trim guy I've ever seen," Richard said. "And I've been here thirty years. I've seen them all. None of them had hands like that."

He was right. Nobody had hands like that.

It wasn't just the trim work. The electrical stuff was where he really shined. Wiring harnesses that looked like spaghetti. Circuits that made no sense to anyone else. Give Doyle a schematic and a multimeter and he'd disappear into a dashboard for hours, emerging with the problem solved and a smug grin on his face.

"It's all just circuits," he'd say. "Electricity wants to flow. You just have to find where it's getting stuck."

Simple when he said it. Impossible when anyone else tried. His hands moved through the wires like they knew them by heart. Testing and probing. Following paths that no one else could see. He'd find shorts that had been hiding for years. He'd trace grounds that seemed impossible. He'd rewire entire systems from memory, no diagrams needed, just his hands and his mind working together like they shared a single brain.

"It's a gift," Pops said once. "Can't teach that. Either you've got it or you don't."

Doyle had it. More than anyone I'd ever seen. The bars were different, but the hands were still there. Two-stepping at Rockin Rodeo, his hands on a woman's waist. The right amount of pressure. The right amount of guidance. Leading without forcing. Moving without thinking.

"Dancing's just like working on cars," he told me once. "You lead with your hands. Your feet follow. But it's the hands that tell the story."

I watched him dance that night. The easy way he moved. The way the girls melted into him. There was something about how he held them. Confident but not aggressive. Present but not possessive. His hands communicated things that words couldn't. Safety, competence and trust.

Girls lined up to dance with him. Not because he was handsome. He wasn't. But because when he held them, they felt something. They felt held. "It's not magic," he said. "It's just paying attention. Feeling what they need and responding to it."

His hands knew things. Things the rest of us had to think about, his hands just did. I remembered the pool at Greenway Parkway. Before everything. When it was just Doyle and Tara in that apartment with the sand they called "the beach." I'd come over sometimes. Watch them together. The way his hands moved when he was with her.

Resting on the small of her back when they stood together. Brushing hair from her face without thinking. Finding her hand across a table. Small touches. Constant touches in a language only they understood.

"I've never had anyone look at me the way she does," he told me once. His hands were rebuilding a carburetor while he talked. Working without looking. Fingers finding the right parts by feel. "She sees me, Hanson. Really sees me."

His hands could do anything. Fix cars, hold women and build a life. They were the best part of him. The truest expression of who he was. Everything good about Doyle was in those hands.

And now. Now they sat in his lap. Curled up and useless. Trapped in gloves that were supposed to help but didn't. Fingers frozen by contractures. Muscles wasted by years of not moving. The hands that could do anything, now unable to do a single thing.

I tried not to look at them but I always did. Every visit my eyes would find them, and I'd remember what they used to be. The man who could trace a wire through a dashboard. The man who could lead a woman across a dance floor. The man who built things, fixed things and touched things with a precision no one else could match. Gone... All of it gone... The gift rotting inside gloves.

He talked about them one day. I hadn't expected it. We'd been talking about the dealership, about some job Richard had mentioned, about nothing important. Then he stopped. Looked down at his hands. And spoke.

"You want to know the worst part?"

I waited.

"It's not the legs. I thought it would be the legs. Not walking or running. Not standing up like a man. But it's not that." He stared at his hands. Those broken, useless hands. "It's these. It's always been these..."

"Doyle..."

"I can feel them." His voice cracked. "That's the cruelest part. The nerves still work, sort of. I can feel them there. Feel them wanting to move. Feel the phantom of what they used to do. But they won't respond. They won't obey. They won't do a single thing they were made to do."

He was crying with the tears running down his face that he couldn't wipe them away.

"I was a man who worked with his hands, Hanson. That's who I was. That's all I was. The trim work. The electrical stuff. The dancing. The women. Everything good about my life came through these hands. And now look at them."

He tried to move his fingers. They barely twitched. "I can't work. I can't touch or hold anyone. They can’t do a single thing they were made to do." His voice was raw. Broken. "They're still there. Still attached and still a part of me but they're dead. They died that night in the pool, even if the rest of me kept going."

I didn't know what to say. There was nothing to say.

"You know what I dream about?"

He asked it a few minutes later. After the tears had dried on his face. After the silence had stretched long enough to become comfortable again.

"No."

"Working on cars... Every night. I'm back at the dealership. Under a hood. Hands deep in an engine. Tracing wires and fixing things. Feeling the grease and the metal and the satisfaction of finding the problem and making it right." He almost smiled. "In my dreams, my hands still work. They do all the things they used to do. And then I wake up."

He looked at me.

"Every morning. Every single morning. That's the hardest part of the day. The moment I wake up and remember. The moment my brain checks in with my body and finds out nothing works. Nothing will ever work again. And I have to live through that realization fresh. Every day. For the rest of my life."

I thought about that. Waking up every day to the same terrible truth. The same loss. The same grief. Over and over for forever.

"I don't know how you do it," I said.

"Neither do I." He closed his eyes. "Some days I don't know why I do it."

The cruelest thing about his injury wasn't the paralysis. It wasn't the wheelchair. It wasn't the facility. It wasn't even the helplessness, the indignity, the dependence on strangers for every basic human function.

It was his hands. The things that had made him who he was, now dead weight at the end of useless arms. The gift he'd been given, rotting away while he watched. The man who could fix anything, unable to fix himself. C4... The fourth cervical vertebra. A tiny piece of bone, a few inches of spinal cord, and everything below it gone. But it was the hands that broke him. The hands that made him grieve his own life while still living it. I left that day with his words in my head. "Can't do a single thing they were made to do."

I thought about Richard. "Those hands of his. God almighty."

I thought about every headliner and wiring harness and two-step and touch. Everything those hands had been. Everything they'd done. Everything they'd meant. Gone now. The man who could do anything, reduced to nothing. The gift that made him who he was, taken away by a moment of drunken stupidity and a few inches of water too shallow for diving. Those hands. God almighty.... Those hands.

Chapter Twenty-One – My Last Visit

I knew it the moment I walked in. Something in the air. Something in the way he looked at me. The calmness from recent weeks was still there, but sharper now. It was more focused now. Like he'd been waiting for this exact day. This exact moment. "Hanson." He smiled when he saw me. A real smile. The kind I hadn't seen since before the accident. "I was hoping you'd come."

"I always come."

"I know." His voice was soft. "Sit down. I want to talk."

He was clear-eyed. Clearer than he'd been in months. The fog of medication seemed to have lifted, or maybe he'd refused his morning pills. Either way, the man looking at me was present... Fully present. The real Doyle, surfacing one more time from the wreckage of what his life had become. "You look good," I said.

"I feel good." He was studying me. Taking me in, like he was memorizing my face. "Really good. For the first time in a long time."

I sat in my chair. The worn seat with the familiar view. The red wheelchair in the corner. How many times had I sat here? How many hours? I joked about how the fabric was permanently indented from my weight. "Tell me about the dealership," he said. "What's going on? What did I miss?"

We talked like we used to. Not the heavy conversations of recent visits. Not the memories and the grief and the slow process of saying goodbye. Just two friends catching up. The dealership, the guys, who was working on what. The jobs that had come in. The funny things that had happened.

"Richard finally retired," I said. "Last month. Thirty-two years and they gave him a gold watch and a handshake."

"A watch? What's he going to do with a watch? Man's never been on time for anything in his life."

I laughed. He laughed and it felt like before.

"Amanda's running the front desk now. You remember Amanda? The one who used to..."

"The one who used to eat Pops' lunch out of the fridge and blame it on Dave." He was smiling. "I remember. Is she still doing that?"

"Pops started writing his name on his sandwiches. In permanent marker. She's eating Dave's lunch now instead."

More laughter. It was easy, natural. Like nothing had changed... Like he wasn't lying in a bed unable to move and I wasn't sitting in a chair waiting for the end.

"Tell me about Lucky's," he said. "Tell me about riding."

I looked at him. "You want to hear about Lucky's?"

"One more time. Tell me about that night. The night you got on the bull."

So, I told him. The smoky arena. The sawdust and the smell of animals. The noise of the crowd. How scared I was, climbing into that chute. How sure I was that I was going to die.

"Three seconds," I said. "That's all I lasted. Three seconds before that thing threw me into the dirt."

"Four if I remember correctly... Longest three or four seconds of your life."

"Yeah, the longest seconds of my life."

He was quiet for a moment while he was remembering with me.

"You know what I told you that night?" he asked.

"You said I had guts."

"I said it takes guts to do something you know you'll fail at." He looked at me. "Most people won't even try. They won't risk looking stupid or won't risk getting hurt. But you climbed on that bull knowing you were going to eat dirt. And you did it anyway."

"I did it because you dared me."

"You did it because that's who you are." His voice was firm. Clear. "You do the hard things, Hanson. Even when they scare you. Even when you know they're going to hurt."

I didn't know what to say to that.

"We had some of the best times in my life."

He said it without warning. Shifting from stories to something else. Something deeper.

"Doyle..."

"Let me finish." His eyes were wet but his voice was steady. "Before the accident and after. Every part of my life that meant anything, you were there. The dealership, the bars and the apartment. All of it. You were a shining star in my life. Before and after."

"You were my brother," I said. The words caught in my throat.

"I was." He nodded. "I was your brother and you were mine. Not because we were blood. Because we chose it. Because every day, we chose each other." He paused. "I never told you that. I never said it out loud. I should have said it a long time ago."

The tears came then. I couldn't stop them.

"Thank you," he said. "For showing up... every week, every time. When everyone else was gone, you kept coming. You kept sitting in that chair and telling me stories and remembering who I used to be. You kept me alive, Hanson. Longer than I would have lasted on my own."

"Don't..."

"I have to." His voice cracked. "I have to say this. While I still can. While I'm still here to say it."

I wanted to tell him not to do it. The words were right there, burning in my chest. Please. There has to be another way. Let me help find someone who can help. Don't leave me alone with this.

But I didn't say any of it. Because I'd made my peace with it, or at least as much peace as anyone could make. He'd decided. He'd been deciding for months, maybe longer. And nothing I said was going to change that. So, I sat there. Let him talk and say the things he needed to say.

"I need you to do something for me," he said.

"What?"

"Live." The word hung in the air. "Really live. Do all the things I was going to do. Have the life I was supposed to have. The shop, the wife and the kids. The garage with the toolbox and the projects that never get finished... All of it." His eyes held mine. "Someone should. Someone should have the life I lost."

"Doyle, I can't..."

"You can." His voice was fierce now. Strong. "You can and you will. Because you're going to walk out of this room and get in your car and drive back to a world that still has possibilities. A world where you can still do things... Build things and love someone... Be someone." He paused. "I'm asking you not to waste it."

I nodded. It was all I could manage.

"Promise me."

"I promise."

He asked me to come closer. I leaned in, close enough to hear him even if he whispered. Close enough to see the tears drying on his face. The hollows where his teeth used to be. The man he'd become. "One more thing," he said.

I waited.

"Don't blame yourself... After. When it happens. Whatever you're thinking right now, about things you could have said or done, about ways you could have stopped me... let it go. This isn't on you. It was never on you. It was always going to end like this."

"Doyle..."

"Promise me that too."

I couldn't speak. Could barely breathe.

"Hanson. Promise me."

"I promise," I whispered. The words felt like stones in my mouth.

And then he did something he'd only done once before.

"Come here," he said.

I didn't understand at first. Then I did. I leaned forward, careful of the tubes and the wires and all the medical equipment keeping him alive. I put my arms around him, as much as I could, given how he was positioned. I held him. The shell of the man he used to be. The brother I was about to lose.

He couldn't hug me back. Not really. His arms didn't work anymore. But I felt him lean into it. Felt the weight of his head against my shoulder. Felt the contact he couldn't make on his own.

"Thank you," he whispered. "For everything. Not just today. Everything."

I held on longer than I should have. Longer than was comfortable. I held on because I knew this was the last time. Because this was goodbye, even if neither of us was saying the word.

The first time we'd hugged was moving day. The day we'd carried furniture into the apartment on Greenway Parkway. It had surprised me. He wasn't a hugger. That's how I knew it meant something. This was the second time, but I didn't know it would be the last time.

I stood up eventually and wiped my face with the back of my hand. I tried to find words that weren't there. "I should go," I said. The most useless thing I could have said.

"Yeah." He was looking at me. That same memorizing look from earlier. Taking me in. Holding on to every detail. "I'll see you next week."

"Yeah." The word caught in my throat. "See you."

Neither of us said goodbye. I walked to the door and turned back. I looked at him one more time in the bed with the wheelchair next to him. The man I'd known since we were young, stupid and working on cars together. "Doyle."

"Yeah?"

I didn't know what to say. There wasn't anything left to say. Everything that mattered had already been said.

"I'm glad you were my friend."

He smiled. The last smile I'd ever see from him. "Me too, Hanson. Me too."

I left him thinking about whatever a man thinks about when he's made the decision Doyle had made. I didn't know. I didn't want to know. I walked down the hallway. Past the nurses' station where the staff who didn't see anything waved goodbye. Past the common room where other patients sat in their wheelchairs, watching TV, waiting for their own endings. Out the door into the parking lot where my car was waiting to take me back to a world he'd never see again.

I sat in the driver's seat for a long time before I started the engine.

This was it. The last visit. I knew it as surely as I'd known anything in my life. He wouldn't be there next week or ever again. What I'd just experienced was the final conversation. The final hug goodbye that neither of us could bring ourselves to say.

I drove home with the weight of the promise I'd made. The life I'd committed to living. The grief that was already beginning, even though he was still alive. See you next week... Neither of us believed it. But we'd said it anyway. Because some lies are kinder than the truth.

Chapter Twenty-Two – The Call

The phone rang at 7:43 in the morning. I was getting ready for work. Coffee half-finished on the counter. Keys in my hand with my mind already at the dealership, thinking about the jobs lined up for the day. It was a normal morning on an ordinary Tuesday. The phone rang and I answered it without looking. "Hanson."

It was Sylvia. Her voice was wrong. Flat in a way that scared me before she said anything else.

"He's gone, Hanson." She paused. A breath that shook. "He's gone."

I sat down. Not because I chose to but because my legs stopped working. The keys fell out of my hand and clattered on the floor somewhere I couldn't see because my vision had gone blurry. Tunnel vision they say... Everything narrowing down to the phone in my hand and the voice on the other end and the words that couldn't be true.

"How?" I heard myself ask. The word came from somewhere far away.

"He fell." Another shaking breath. "Sometime in the night. They found him this morning. Face down on the floor." She was crying now. The flat tone cracking into something raw. "He must have thrown himself forward out of the bed. He landed on his chest face down. And then..."

She didn't finish. She didn't have to. I understood. No gun... No knife... No help from anyone. Just his body, gravity and the floor. He'd found a way after all. I don't remember the call ending.

One moment I was listening to Sylvia cry, the next I was sitting in silence with a dead phone in my hand. The coffee was getting cold on the counter. My keys were still on the floor. The world outside was still going on, cars driving past, birds singing, sun rising, like nothing had happened. But everything had happened. He was gone. Really gone... Not dying slowly in that bed or fading away visit by visit. He was gone... The word didn't make sense. Gone where? Gone how? Gone from a world that had already taken everything from him, that had stripped him down to nothing and left him with no choice except this one. I picked up my keys. I don't know why. Force of habit. My brain couldn't process what had happened, so it defaulted to routine. Keys.... Car... Work. The same things I did every day. As if today was every day. As if everything hadn't changed.

I drove not to work and not anywhere specific. I just drove mindlessly as the city was unspooling around me, streets I knew by heart turning into streets I didn't recognize. My eyes were open, but I wasn't seeing anything. It was just the road ahead with the white line. Just the next turn and the next and the next. He'd done it.

The thing I'd known was coming. The thing I'd watched him prepare for. The thing he'd told me about without telling me, the peace that was worse than desperation. He'd done it and I'd let him. I'd known it was coming, and I hadn't stopped it and now he was dead.

I pulled over somewhere. It was a parking lot or a side street. I don't remember. I put my head on the steering wheel and I let it come. The grief filled with guilt. The finality of it all...

The complicated mess of emotions that didn't have names. Relief that he wasn't suffering anymore. Anger over everything that happened to him. Shame that I felt either of those things.

I don't recall if there was a funeral... If there was, I should have attended. He was a friend who I called my brother. I should have been there. I should have stood in some church or funeral home and said goodbye properly. Done the thing you're supposed to do.

I couldn't explain it then and I can barely explain it now. Something about seeing him like that. In a box, done up in makeup to look like he was sleeping. People would be talking about him like he was already history. Already a memory instead of a person who lived.

I couldn't face it or the other people who would be there, the relatives, acquaintances and strangers who would all have their own version of who Doyle was. Their own grief with their own claim on him. I'd had my goodbye in that room. In that hug and in the promise I'd made. A funeral wasn't going to give me anything I didn't already have.

My grandmother was surprised to see me three days later. I was at her house. I don't remember driving there. I don't remember deciding to go but that's where I ended up, sitting at her kitchen table like I had when I was a kid, staring at nothing while she made tea I wasn't going to drink.

She was old. Old enough that she'd buried her husband and two of her children. Old enough that death had stopped being a stranger.

"You lost someone," she said. Not a question.

I nodded.

"Someone important."

Another nod. She poured the tea anyway. She set the cup in front of me and sat down across the table with the same arthritic grace she'd always had. Patient and waiting.

"I don't know what to do," I said finally. "I don't know how to do this."

"There's no how." She wrapped her hands around her own cup.

"There's just doing. Living through it. Getting up every day even when you don't want to."

"It hurts."

"It's supposed to." Her eyes were kind. Knowing. "That's how you know it mattered. If it didn't hurt, it wouldn't have been real."

I looked at her. This woman who had outlived so many people. Who had buried, grieved and kept going, over and over. How did she do it? How did anyone do it? "Mind the grief, boy," she said softly. "It can take you too. If you let it."

The words stayed with me. Mind the grief... It can take you too.

I watched my grandmother. The way she moved through her days. Slow and deliberate. She was still finding reasons to get up. Still finding things that mattered. She'd lost people too. She lost more than I could count. But she was still here. Still drinking tea and making bread while watching the sun set over the valley. Grief didn't have to be the end. That's what she was showing me. It could be carried... It could be survived. You could live with a hole in your chest and still live.

Work was the hardest. Walking back into the dealership three days after the call. Everyone knew. News traveled fast in places like that. The guys who'd worked with Doyle, the ones who remembered him before, they all looked at me with that same careful expression. Pity and sympathy. Not knowing what to say.

Pops was the only one who said anything. He caught me in the break room. The coffee machine humming between us. His face lined with decades of grease and sun with grief of his own.

"Best trim guy I ever worked with," he said. "Those hands of his." He shook his head. "He had that something..."

I nodded. I couldn't speak.

"Nothing anyone could have done," Pops said. "You know that, right? Nothing anyone could have done to change how things went. Some roads only go one direction."

"I know."

"Do you?" He looked at me. Really looked. "Because I've seen men eat themselves alive with guilt over things they couldn't control. Don't be one of them. He wouldn't have wanted that."

He squeezed my shoulder and walked away. He didn't say anything else. He didn't need to. Pops had never been so nice to me and that day I respected him more than I would ever have admitted.

The grief came in waves. Some days I was fine and functional. I was getting through the work, going through the motions, almost forgetting for whole hours at a time. Then something would trigger it. A song on the radio. A Lincoln pulling into the lot. Someone laughing in that particular way Doyle used to laugh.

And the wave would hit. It would knock me sideways. Leave me gasping in my car, the bathroom or some corner of the shop where no one could see me fall apart. I learned to ride it out and let it come and let it go. To know that it would pass, eventually, even when it felt like drowning.

The bars were the worst. All the places we used to go together. It took a while to be able to go there again. When I did, the smoke and the music took me back. I stopped going out for a bit. I had stopped trying to find the person I used to be in the places we used to be together. That person was gone too. Buried somewhere I couldn't find him. Instead, I found a new wingman named Maverick. He was one of Doyle's friends and we kinda picked up where he left it. He was something and he knew Doyle's language. It was therapeutic for both of us in a way.

As Mav would say, let's go clubbing and hang up the hat for a while. Mav was just about as crazy as Doyle but he didn't have the charm. We had to work the room so much harder than Doyle ever did. We would speak of Doyle like he was a living legend but outside of that I stopped talking about him.

Not right away. At first people asked the usual questions. You know the coworkers and acquaintances circle. People who knew we'd been close. "How are you holding up?" "Are you okay?" "If you need to talk..."

I said the right things. I'm fine and I'm getting better. Thanks for asking. But I didn't actually talk about him. I didn't say his name, and I didn't share the memories, the grief or anything real.

It was easier that way. Safer... Talking about him made him real again, and when he was real, the loss was real too. If I didn't talk about him, I could keep the grief at a distance where it was manageable and survivable.

Days turned into weeks. Weeks into months. Months into years. They eventually replaced him at the dealership and the new guy was ok but he didn't have half the talent Doyle did. And I relished that fact as I continued to give Pops a rash of shit.

It was twenty years before I spoke his name to anyone outside of those who knew him. Even Maverick and I only brought him up every once in a blue moon. But other than that, not to anyone real. Not out loud or in any way that mattered. He lived in my head, in my memories, in the quiet moments when I let myself remember. But I never talked about him. I never told anyone who he was or how he died. The grief didn't go away. It just went underground. It settled into my bones like an old injury that aches when the weather changes. I learned to live with it and build around it. I carried it without letting it carry me.

I never found out where they put him. The funeral I didn't attend. The grave site I never visited. The final resting place of the man who was my brother. Somewhere out there, there's a headstone with his name on it. Or maybe just a plaque... Or maybe nothing at all. I don't know. I could have asked. I could have found out, but I didn't.

Maybe because it didn't matter. He wasn't there, wherever they put him. The real Doyle had left that body a long time before it stopped breathing. The real Doyle was in the memories in the stories; at the bars we used to visit and the cars we used to fix along with the women we used to chase with the life we used to live.

I never found out where they put him and somehow, that was okay.

I learned to carry it. That's the thing about grief. You don't put it down. You don't get over it. You don't move on in the way people say you should. You just get stronger. The weight stays the same, but you build the muscle to carry it. Day after day. Year after year. Until it becomes part of you. Until you can't remember what it felt like to walk around without it. He would have been proud of me, I think. I kept my promise. I lived. Not perfectly or the way he would have wanted, maybe. But I lived. I got up every day and went to work. I built something and I found reasons to keep going even when I didn't want to. I carried the weight of him. The memory of him and I didn't let it take me. Mind the grief, boy. It can take you too but it didn't. I made sure of that.

Epilogue - Twenty Years Later

Beth didn't say anything for a long time. We sat there in the quiet of our bedroom, the lamp casting soft light across her face, my words still hanging in the air between us. I had told her the full story... All of it. Twenty years of silence finally broken. She reached over and took my hand. "Thank you," she said. "For telling me."

I didn't know what I'd expected. Questions, maybe. Judgment. The look people get when they realize you've been carrying something they didn't know about. But she just held my hand and let the silence stretch. She let me breathe.

"I didn't know how to tell you," I said. "I didn't know how to explain it. Any of it."

"You don't have to explain." She squeezed my hand. "I understand now about the pools. The way you look sometimes, when you think I'm not watching. The part of you that always seemed locked away." She paused. "I always knew there was something. I just didn't know what."

I thought about that. The locked room. That's how she'd described it once, years ago. The part of me I kept hidden. She'd never demanded the key. She never pushed or made me feel like I owed her access to every corner of who I was and I loved her for that.

"You could have asked," I said. "Any time. You could have pushed."

"I know." She was looking at me in that way she had. Seeing me. Really seeing me. "But some doors need to be opened from the inside. If I'd forced my way in, it wouldn't have been the same."

"What made you ask tonight?"

She smiled. A small, sad smile. "It was the news... and I also received a pool party invitation. The way your face changed when you saw the news. I've seen that look before, but never quite so... raw. I thought maybe you were finally ready."

I was finally ready. Twenty years... That's how long it took. Twenty years of carrying him alone. Of keeping the story locked away where no one could see it. Of living my life in the present while a part of me stayed forever in the past but I'd kept my promise.

I stayed at the dealership and made service writer eventually. I never opened my own shop, but that was okay. The shop had been his dream, not mine. I found my own version of success that came out to be steady work with good people. A life that fit and I found Beth.

She came into the dealership five years after Doyle died. She had a Classic Mustang that needed a tune. Her highlighted hair and smart eyes were hard to miss. Something about her that made me look twice. "I know nothing about cars," she said or so she claimed... "So please don't try to sell me anything I don't need."

I laughed. "Fair enough."

I was honest with her. I even gave her a discount. She looked at me like she was trying to figure out my angle. "Most places would have found something wrong," she said.

"Most places are trying to make money off you. I'm just trying to help."

She came back a week later. Not for the car... but for me.

We got married three years after that. Small ceremony with just family and a few friends. I thought about Doyle that day. I wondered if he was watching somehow. I wondered what he'd think of her.

He would have liked Beth. He would have given me shit about marrying a Mustang driver. He would have made some joke about finally finding someone willing to put up with me.

You would have liked her; I told him in my head. She sees me. Really sees me. The way Tara saw you, before everything went wrong. But he wasn't there. That was the hardest part. The absence where he should have been. Standing up with me. Making inappropriate jokes. Being my best man the way he'd been my best friend. He wasn't there but he was.

In the promises I'd kept. In the life I'd built. In the man I'd become because he'd asked me to really live.

"You never told anyone," Beth said.

"No."

"Why?"

I thought about how to answer. There were so many reasons. The grief that had swallowed me whole in those early days. The guilt that still flickered sometimes, even now. The way talking about him made him real again, and when he was real, losing him was real too. But that wasn't the whole truth.

"Because it was ours," I said finally. "Mine and his. The bars. The dealership. That night I rode the bull. The way he could light up a room just by walking into it. All of it." I paused. "Sharing it felt like giving it away. Letting strangers into my past."

"But you told me."

"You're not a stranger." I looked at her. This woman who had loved me for years without knowing this part of me. Who had given me the space to keep my secrets while never making me feel like they divided us. "You're my wife. And you deserved to know."

She leaned over and kissed my cheek.

"He sounds like he was something special."

"He was." My voice caught. Even after twenty years, it still caught. "He really was. And I found out years later from Maverick that Tara and him did get a chance to meet up. Doyle was able to sort it out in his way. I was happy to hear that."

She asked about the pools. I knew she would. That's what had started all of this. She wasn't sure how to present it, but she showed me the invitation to her coworker's pool party. The way I'd looked at it like it was challenging but it had been long enough.

"I think I can make it," I said.

"You don't have to if you don't want too."

"I want to." I took a breath. "It's not fear. Not exactly. It's more like... they're kinda haunted now. Sometimes when I look at them, I see... I see that one. The one with the sand he called the beach. The shallow end where he dove in and never came out the same."

She was quiet for a moment.

"We don't have to go to the party."

"I know."

"And I'll never ask you to go to a pool party again."

"I know that too." I squeezed her hand. "But thank you. For understanding. For not thinking I'm crazy."

"You're not crazy." Her voice was firm. "You're someone who lost his someone in a terrible way and can't look at the thing that took him. That's not crazy. That's human."

We sat there for a while longer with the lamp in the quiet. The weight of everything I'd finally said out loud. Twenty years of carrying it alone, and now someone else knew. Someone else could help hold it.

"Do you feel better?" she asked.

I thought about it. Did I feel better? The grief was still there. The memories. The ghost of him that would never fully leave. But something had shifted. Something had loosened. "Yeah," I said. "I think I do."

"Good." She yawned. It was late. The story had taken hours to tell. "Come to bed."

"In a minute."

She kissed me again and went to lie down. I heard the sheets rustle as she got comfortable. I heard her breathing start to slow. I stayed up for a while. Looking at nothing. Thinking about everything. His name was Robert Doyle.

He was a trim guy at a Ford dealership in Phoenix. He could fix any electrical problem, no matter how impossible. He could two-step like nobody's business and make any woman feel like she was the only person in the room. He had hands that could do anything and a smile that could light up the darkest bar.

He dove into a pool one night and broke his neck. He spent years trapped in a body that didn't work anymore. I watched everything he was get stripped away piece by piece until there was nothing left but the waiting. And then he ended it. On his own terms. The only way he had left.

I don't dive into pools anymore and now you know why.

THE END

References

A Documentary Resource for Readers of *The Shallow End*

The following information is provided to inform readers about spinal injuries that result from diving or pool accidents.

C4 Spinal Cord Injuries in the United States

Diving into shallow water represents one of the most preventable yet devastating causes of spinal cord injury (SCI) in the United States. Each year, approximately 800 Americans are permanently paralyzed as a result of diving accidents, with half of these injuries resulting in quadriplegia (Help Hope Live). Diving remains the single largest cause of sports-related spinal cord injuries, and the cervical spine, particularly the C4-C6 vertebrae—bears the overwhelming majority of this trauma.

This document examines the epidemiology of C4 spinal cord injuries resulting from pool and diving accidents, the profound impact on survivors, and the promising medical advances that may one day restore function to those living with these catastrophic injuries.

According to the National Spinal Cord Injury Statistical Center, between three and five percent of all spinal cord injuries in the United States occur as a result of swimming or diving accidents (Biren Law). While this percentage may seem modest, the severity of these injuries and their concentration among young, healthy individuals makes them particularly tragic.

A comprehensive study analyzing data from over 161 million patients between 2010 and 2021 identified 3,829 individuals who suffered diving-related spine injuries (DRSIs) in the United States (Engel-Haber et al.). Of these cases:

- The cervical spine was involved in 53% of injuries
- 629 patients (16.4%) sustained spinal cord injuries resulting in paralysis
- The rate of diving-related spine injuries has significantly decreased in recent years

The fourth cervical vertebra (C4) represents a critical anatomical threshold. Injuries at this level result in quadriplegia (paralysis of all four limbs) with patients retaining only limited shoulder and bicep function. One study of 34 diving accident patients found that C4 was the most common neurologic level of injury, affecting 39.4% of patients (Aito et al.). Additional research confirms that on hospital admission, the level of paralysis was at C4 in 31.9% of cases and C5 in 33.7% (Aito et al.).

The majority of diving-related cervical injuries occur in the mid to low cervical spinal column (C5-C6 vertebrae), a region particularly susceptible to fractures due to its biomechanical mobility (Barss et al.).

Diving injuries demonstrate remarkably consistent demographic patterns across multiple international studies

- **Gender**: Males account for 86-97% of all diving-related spinal cord injuries (Kiwerski; Barss et al.)

- **Age**: Mean age ranges from 24-27 years, representing young adults in their physical prime (Barss et al.)
- **Seasonality**: 88-90% of accidents occur during summer months, between May and August (Aito et al.)
- **Location**: Swimming pools in holiday lodges account for 36.4% of injuries; inland waters account for 56.2% (Aito et al.; Kiwerski)

Alcohol intoxication plays a significant role in diving accidents. One Polish study found that 15 out of 18 diving-related spinal cord injury cases involved alcohol intoxication (Kiwerski). Impaired judgment leads individuals to dive into unfamiliar waters without assessing depth, ignore warning signs, and overestimate their physical abilities.

Eighty-five percent of spinal cord injuries from diving occur in shallow water, typically at depths of less than 1.4 meters (Grossman Roth). The mechanism involves hyperflexion or axial loading of the cervical spine when the head strikes the bottom surface. This sudden deceleration and compression causes vertebral fractures and, critically, damage to the delicate spinal cord tissue within.

A complete C4 spinal cord injury results in

- **Paralysis**: Loss of all motor function below the shoulders
- **Respiratory compromise**: Diaphragm function may be impaired, potentially requiring ventilator support
- **Loss of hand function**: Complete inability to grip, manipulate objects, or perform fine motor tasks

- **Autonomic dysfunction**: Impaired regulation of blood pressure, body temperature, bladder, and bowel function
- **Sensory loss**: Absence of sensation below the level of injury

Patients retain head and neck control, limited shoulder movement, and potentially some bicep function, but cannot independently perform activities of daily living such as eating, dressing, or personal hygiene.

The financial burden of spinal cord injury is staggering. One European study calculated the mean direct cost for a patient with a complete injury (ASIA class A) at approximately 300,000 Euros, compared to around 10,000 Euros for patients with less severe injuries (Aito et al.).

Beyond financial costs, the personal toll is profound. The same study documented 11 divorces and 7 job losses among their patient cohort (Aito et al.). Full fitness recovery was achieved in only 22% of diving-related spinal injury cases in one study, with the remainder facing permanent disability (Kiwerski).

The sudden transition from able-bodied to quadriplegic creates immense psychological trauma. Depression, anxiety, and suicidal ideation are significantly elevated in the SCI population, particularly among those injured young who face decades of dependency and limitation.

Current Standard of Care

Present treatment for C4 spinal cord injuries focuses on:

1. **Acute stabilization**: Surgical decompression and spinal fusion to

prevent further damage

2. **Rehabilitation**: Physical and occupational therapy to maximize remaining function

3. **Supportive care**: Management of complications including respiratory support, pressure ulcer prevention, and autonomic dysreflexia

4. **Assistive technology**: Power wheelchairs, environmental controls, and communication devices

While these interventions improve quality of life, they do not restore lost neurological function. However, several emerging therapies offer hope for future recovery.

Stem Cell Therapy

Cell transplantation has emerged as one of the most promising approaches to spinal cord injury treatment. Over the past decade, numerous clinical studies have investigated various cell types including fetal neural stem/progenitor cells (NS/PCs), pluripotent stem cell-derived NS/PCs, mesenchymal stem/stromal cells (MSCs), and olfactory ensheathing cells (Huang et al.).

Current Status:

No FDA-approved stem cell therapies are currently available for spinal cord injuries in the United States

- One MSC-based therapy has received conditional approval in Japan (Huang et al.)

- Keio University initiated the first clinical study using induced pluripotent stem (iPS) cells in 2020, with completion reported in November 2024 and no serious adverse effects observed (Huang et al.)

Transplanted mesenchymal stem cells are believed to work by homing to damaged sites and inducing neurotrophic and protective effects. MSCs contribute to neuroprotection by stabilizing the blood-spinal cord barrier and creating an environment permissive to nerve regeneration and remyelination (Huang et al.).

A 2023 case report documented a 41-year-old quadriplegic patient who received multiple intravenous infusions of autologous adipose-derived mesenchymal stem cells. While dramatic recovery was not observed, MRI imaging showed subtle improvement with a decrease in T2 abnormality (Wahyuni et al.).

In December 2024, researchers at the University of California San Diego published findings demonstrating that neural stem cell transplantation shows particular promise for treating chronic spinal cord injury—offering hope to patients years after their initial trauma (UC San Diego Health).

Epidural spinal cord stimulation (ESCS) represents perhaps the most exciting breakthrough in SCI treatment. Unlike rehabilitation strategies requiring retained motor ability, ESCS has demonstrated the capacity to restore volitional motor control even in motor-complete patients (Angeli et al.).

Surgically implanted electrodes deliver electrical stimulation to the lumbosacral spinal cord, activating motor neurons below the level of injury. When combined with intensive rehabilitation, this stimulation can partially restore:

- Standing ability
- Stepping and walking function
- Cardiovascular regulation
- Bladder and bowel function (Rowald et al.)

A landmark clinical study (STIMO, ClinicalTrials.gov: NCT02936453) employed electrode arrays positioned near dorsal roots in three individuals with chronic, sensorimotor complete cervical SCI. All three participants achieved stepping function, eventually reaching walking speeds between 0.1 and 0.25 m/s. In six-minute walk tests, participants ambulated 25, 35, and 75 meters respectively (Rowald et al.).

A 2025 pilot study implanted 32-contact epidural stimulators in three participants with chronic, sensorimotor complete thoracic SCI. All participants achieved independent standing through stimulation-enabled muscle activation, despite the complete absence of voluntary movement prior to treatment (Herrity et al.).

Recent research published in *Science Translational Medicine* demonstrated that combining high-frequency epidural electrical stimulation (HF-EES) with low-frequency stimulation and intensive rehabilitation produced notable improvements in lower limb kinematics, muscle strength, and clinical motor assessments (Barraud et al.).

The future of SCI treatment likely lies in combinatorial approaches:

Pharmacological agents: Riluzole, minocycline, and other neuroprotective drugs

Molecular targeting: Anti-Nogo-A antibodies that block regeneration inhibitors

Brain-computer interfaces: Direct neural control of assistive devices and potentially stimulation systems

Bioengineered scaffolds: Providing structural support for nerve regeneration

Gene therapy: Modifying cellular responses to promote regeneration

Despite promising results, significant challenges remain:

1. **Small sample sizes**: Most clinical studies involve fewer than 20 patients

2. **Patient heterogeneity**: Wide variation in injury level, completeness, and chronicity

3. **Regulatory hurdles**: FDA approval requires extensive safety and efficacy data

4. **Cost**: Experimental treatments remain prohibitively expensive

5. **Chronic vs. acute**: Most research focuses on acute injuries; chronic patients face additional scar tissue barriers

Experts suggest that meaningful clinical applications of regenerative therapies may emerge within the next decade, though complete functional restoration remains a longer-term goal.

Prevention

Given the devastating and largely irreversible nature of diving-related spinal cord injuries, prevention remains paramount

Education: Public awareness campaigns about shallow water dangers

Signage: Clear "No Diving" warnings at pools and natural water bodies

Supervision: Trained lifeguards and responsible adult oversight

Alcohol awareness: Understanding that intoxication dramatically increases risk

Feet-first entry: Teaching safe water entry techniques

Depth assessment: Always checking water depth before entering

C4 spinal cord injuries from diving accidents represent a preventable tragedy that continues to devastate hundreds of American families each year. While current medical care focuses on managing complications and maximizing remaining function, emerging technologies offer genuine hope for the future.

Stem cell therapies, epidural stimulation, and combinatorial approaches are moving from laboratory proof-of-concept to human clinical trials. For the first time in history, patients with complete spinal cord injuries are regaining voluntary movement through these experimental interventions.

Though FDA-approved therapies remain years away, the trajectory of research suggests that individuals injured today may eventually benefit from treatments currently in development. The shallow end that takes so much may not have the final word.

Works Cited

Aito, Sergio, et al. "Cervical Spine Injuries Resulting from Diving Accidents in Swimming Pools: Outcome of 34 Patients." *European Spine Journal*, vol. 19, no. 4, 2010, pp. 552-557. PMC, https://pmc.ncbi.nlm.nih.gov/articles/PMC2899837/

Angeli, Claudia A., et al. "Recovery of Over-Ground Walking after Chronic Motor Complete Spinal Cord Injury." *New England Journal of Medicine*, vol. 379, 2018, pp. 1244-1250.

Barraud, Quentin, et al. "High-Frequency Epidural Electrical Stimulation Reduces Spasticity and Facilitates Walking Recovery in Patients with Spinal Cord Injury." *Science Translational Medicine*, vol. 16, 2024. https://www.science.org/doi/10.1126/scitranslmed.adp9607

Barss, Peter, et al. "An Overview of Spinal Injuries due to Dive or Fall into Shallow Water: Our Long-Term, Double-Center Experience from the Aegean Coast." *World Neurosurgery*, vol. 151, 2021, pp. e651-e660. PMC, https://pmc.ncbi.nlm.nih.gov/articles/PMC8192199/

Biren Law. "Swimming Pools Are a Source of Spinal Cord Injuries." *Biren Law*, https://biren.com/swimming-pools-are-a-source-of-spinal-cord-injuries/

Engel-Haber, Einat, et al. "The Incidence and Trends of Diving-Related Spine Injuries in the United States and Risk Factors Associated with

Spinal Cord Injury." *Spinal Cord*, 2025. https://www.nature.com/articles/s41393-025-01098-6

Grossman Roth. "Don't Dive In: The Hidden Dangers of Shallow Water and Spinal Cord Injuries." *Grossman Roth Yaffa Cohen*, https://www.grossmanroth.com/p/102kbob/dont-dive-in-the-hidden-dangers-of-shallow-water-and-spinal-cord-injuries/

Help Hope Live. "5 Unforgettable Facts About Diving and Spinal Cord Injuries." *Help Hope Live*, https://helphopelive.org/diving-paralysis-spinal-cord-injury-statistics/

Herrity, April N., et al. "Effect of Epidural Spinal Cord Stimulation in Individuals with Sensorimotor Complete Spinal Cord Injury: A Pilot Study." *Frontiers in Systems Neuroscience*, vol. 19, 2025. https://www.frontiersin.org/journals/systems-neuroscience/articles/10.3389/fnsys.2025.1622033/full

Huang, He, et al. "Stem Cell Therapies for Spinal Cord Injury in Humans: A Review of Recent Clinical Research." *Neural Regeneration Research*, vol. 20, 2025. PMC, https://pmc.ncbi.nlm.nih.gov/articles/PMC11870206/

Kiwerski, Jerzy. "Spinal Cord Injuries Due to Diving Accidents." *Spinal Cord*, vol. 17, 1979, pp. 311-314. https://www.nature.com/articles/3101695

Mayo Clinic. "Spinal Cord Injury Epidural Stimulation." *Mayo Clinic Clinical Trials*, https://www.mayo.edu/research/clinical-trials/cls-20167853

Rowald, Andreas, et al. "Activity-Dependent Spinal Cord Neuromodulation Rapidly Restores Trunk and Leg Motor Functions after Complete Paralysis." *Nature Medicine*, vol. 28, 2022, pp. 260-271.

UC San Diego Health. "Neural Stem Cell Transplantation Shows Promise for Treating Chronic Spinal Cord Injury." *ScienceDaily*, 17 Dec. 2024, https://www.sciencedaily.com/releases/2024/12/241217131102.htm

Wahyuni, Luh Karunia, et al. "Functional Recovery of a 41-Year-Old Quadriplegic Spinal Cord Injury Patient Following Multiple Intravenous Infusions of Autologous Adipose-Derived Mesenchymal Stem Cells: A Case Report." *Frontiers in Transplantation*, vol. 2, 2023. https://www.frontiersin.org/journals/transplantation/articles/10.3389/frtra.2023.1287508/full

Similar books by the author with a Christian theme can be found at:

Amazon.com/author/rtg

Made in the USA
Coppell, TX
20 January 2026

68850041R00163